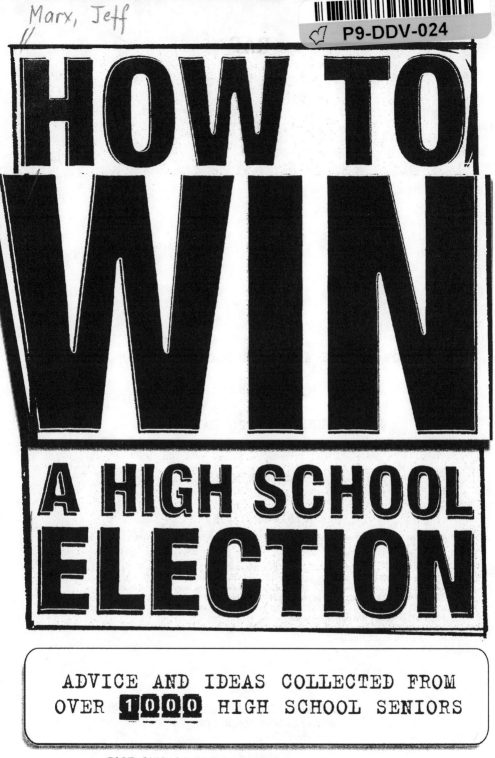

HOW TO WIN
A HIGH SCHOOL
ELECTION

ADVICE AND IDEAS COLLECTED FROM
OVER **1000** HIGH SCHOOL SENIORS

HOW TO WIN A HIGH SCHOOL ELECTION

by JEFF MARX

COVER DESIGN BY JORDAN ATLAS

FIRST EDITION

CONTACT:

publisher@schoolelection.com
www.schoolelection.com

ISBN 0-966-7824-0-2

Printed in the United States of America

Tremendous thanks to all the 1,000+ students
who answered my email with input for this book.

You have taught me so much.

May all the good you do come back to you.

For Richard McGlothlin,
who encouraged me when nobody else did.

So shines a good deed in a naughty world.

The only thing to do with good advice is pass it on.
It is never any use to oneself.

Oscar Wilde

Write in this book. Make it your own.

———————————————

Doggie-ear the pages.

Circle things you like.

Draw in the margins.

———————————————

You can always buy another copy.

PREFACE

Yes, school elections are usually popularity contests.

But *anyone can win*. You don't need to be popular.

You're a voter—do you choose one candidate over another *because* he or she is popular?

School elections are not necessarily won by the candidate who's the best-looking, who's the best athlete, who's the smartest, who has the highest grades, who's the most talented, who has the most experience, who's the funniest, who dresses most expensively, who throws the biggest parties, or who has the most friends.

It's not about having the biggest or the most posters, or about spending the most money on handing out candy, or about giving the most intelligent and professional speech, or even about having the best ideas or being most qualified for the office.

Winning a high school election all comes down to four things:

1. THE RIGHT ATTITUDE

2. A GREAT SPEECH

3. TALKING TO PEOPLE AND ASKING THEM TO VOTE

4. GETTING YOUR NAME REMEMBERED

Voters' minds are almost always made up during the campaign period, not before.

Anyone who is sincere and appealing can win.

In fact, people who seem less likely to win can actually have a much *better* chance of winning than the more popular people, if they want it more, try harder, and take care to do it right.

Nobody really likes voting for the same old people, especially when they become full of themselves and start thinking they're somehow better than everyone else.

It's not about who's *popular,* it's about who's *well-liked.* There's a huge difference.

It doesn't matter whether you're popular or not, well-known or not, or experienced or not. If you genuinely want to be elected into office for the right reasons, and if you're willing to take some risks in putting yourself "out there" and sincerely asking people to support you, *you can get enough votes to win.*

Underdogs win all the time.

Here's how.

CONTENTS

IDEAS FOR SPEECHES AND POSTERS

MORE ADVICE FROM YOUR PEERS

> ➤ You don't need to be popular to win a school election.

> ➤ Students get tired of seeing the same people always win.

> ➤ You absolutely can't win if you don't try.

> ➤ BE YOURSELF! Be honest, be sincere, be genuine.

> ➤ Be a friendly "people person" and talk to everyone.

> ➤ Start as EARLY as possible!

> ➤ Strive to be a peer, not a politician.

> ➤ Don't try to make your opponents look bad. It just makes you look like a jerk.

> ➤ Be confident and positive, but don't get cocky or arrogant.

A Great Speech

> ➢ Don't be overly serious.

> ➢ You're not being graded. Remember why you're there and who you're talking to.

> ➢ Don't expect your speech to miraculously come together while you're up there. Prepare and practice it beforehand!

> ➢ To be comfortable and natural while speaking in front of an audience, just speak from the heart about what you're saying, and don't worry about speaking "correctly."

> ➢ Some ways to be more comfortable while giving a speech

> ➢ The confidence you demonstrate while you're speaking is just as important as what you're saying.

> ➢ Don't list everything you've ever done—nobody cares. Keep it SHORT, or you'll lose your audience.

> ➢ Talk about real issues and what you plan to do for the school.

> ➢ But don't promise something you can't deliver.

> ➢ Most campaign speeches are boring. Make yours fun!

> ➢ There's a difference between being funny and being stupid. Don't make your whole campaign into a joke, and don't do something you'll be embarrassed if people remember.

Talk to People and Ask Them to Vote

> ➢ It's the STUDENTS who will be voting. Go meet them!

> ➢ You don't have to be friends with everyone to be friendly.

> ➢ Be aware of what voters want. Ask them. Listen to them.

> ➢ Not everyone votes. Go after the ones who don't. If you ask them to vote, you're asking them to do you a favor.

> ➢ Get people involved in helping your campaign.

Getting Your Name Remembered

PART 4

FINAL NOTE

WHY THIS BOOK
(The Author's Story)

When I was a Junior in high school, I decided to run for Vice-President of the Student Council. I had no experience as a class officer or Student Council member, I wasn't popular, and the other two candidates were far more qualified than I was. One was a popular cheerleader and multiple-term class officer, the other was a top student who had held Student Council positions for years, was already the Student Council Secretary, and was widely expected to win. I was the underdog.

I decided to come up with a real "issue" that I could run with. I looked around the school and thought to myself, "What could a Student Council officer do to make this school a better place to be?" I decided that the school rule prohibiting students from ordering pizza deliveries at lunchtime was worth addressing. So I went to the principal and discussed the issue with him, and he explained to me that the rule was made years ago because students were leaving their pizza boxes all over school, creating a mess. I asked him if we could have a "trial period" where we could try allowing them again, on the condition that the school remained clean. He agreed.

I then called up the local pizza place and asked the manager if we could get a special deal for students. We worked out a cheap special, and planned to print discount coupons. I unveiled the plan in my campaign speech, as an example of the kind of thing I would do in office, not just talk about. I said it was already done, showing that I'm the kind of person who *gets things done* rather than just making promises.

The stodgy old Student Council advisor didn't like this one bit, and he talked the principal out of fulfilling his promise to me. (Among other things, he said that if anyone was going to sell pizza during lunchtime, it should be the Student Council's student store, not the local pizza delivery place.) Between him and the principal, they reneged on me and then made sure the entire student body knew that my campaign promise would not be kept, and that I had "lied" in my speech. They had notices to this effect read to each class during the morning announcements and they put flyers up on the walls and doors of the cafeteria. They even put signs saying this right on the doors of the voting area. It was devastating. They made me look like a liar even though I honestly had promised only what the principal assured me I could.

Despite this, how did I win?

Well, instead of turning red and crawling under a rock, or dropping out of the race, I took this as an opportunity to meet people and talk to them. I hung around the hallways and the cafeteria, and I said hello to everyone I saw and asked him or her to vote. Almost every single person asked me what had happened with the pizza, and I took the time and care to explain the whole story to each and every person who was interested. I said, "I tried. The principal promised me we could do it, and then he changed his mind. Now they've made me look like a liar. Do you really think I would have gotten up there and flat-out lied?"

I'm convinced that my "damage control" efforts in talking to everyone who would listen was what won me support. I think that on an individual, one-on-one basis, I showed a lot of students that I was friendly, genuine, caring, passionate, and down-to-earth.

And, very importantly, I asked each of them—knowing that every vote was important—to please be sure to vote.

I had an aggressive underdog mentality. I felt I was the candidate least likely to win, so I tried harder than my opponents.

During my speech, I was confident and enthusiastic about the pizza and my desire to do something to make the school better. It was obvious that I was talking about something I was genuinely excited about.

On the other hand, one of my opponents got mad at the audience's inattention during her speech and started demanding, "Listen to me! Listen to me!" (which only made the audience laugh at her). The other opponent tried to make her competition look bad by calling us names ("Little Miss Cheerleader here and The Pizza Man"), which was not admired by anyone.

Who could have predicted it? Each of my popular, well-qualified opponents had done something stupid, sabotaging their chances of winning, and I was out there talking to the students and trying to get one vote at a time.

In the end, even though my pizza plan didn't come through, I think I succeeded in letting everyone know that I was trying to do something good for the school, and that I was a sincere person who would do whatever I could to serve the student body.

Also—this is crucially important—I recognized that not everyone votes. *Often, the candidate who wins is not necessarily the one with the most widespread support, but the one who gets the most people to actually go cast ballots.* I did. I pleaded with people to go cast a vote, confident that if I was merely asking them nicely to "at least go make a choice" instead of pressuring them only to "vote for me," most of the people I asked would probably vote for me anyway.

It's all about people. It's NOT about being slick and political, kissing babies, and putting up posters; it's about being friendly, being genuine, being confident, and getting people to the polls.

If I could win a high school election, *ANYBODY* can.

If you're interested at all in doing the job, go for it! Nobody knows what you want except you, and nobody will be as sorry as you if you don't go after it. So don't stop yourself!

Your chances of winning are far better than you'd imagine.

PART 1

SUMMARY

AND

BEST ADVICE

SHOULD YOU RUN?

You don't need to be popular to win a school election.

In fact, most of your class probably secretly resents the popular people with the snotty I'm-better-than-you-and-nobody-can-beat-me attitudes, and would be glad to vote for anyone with the courage to run against them.*

Students get tired of seeing the same old people win again and again. People grow and change. They like giving "new blood" a chance whenever possible—perhaps hoping that someday they'll get a chance too.

Also, everyone likes to prove that it's possible to be a nice person and succeed. Students will *only* vote for someone they *like*. The popular people don't always fit into that category.

Don't think that behaving like you're a shoo-in will win you votes. Whether you're popular or not, you should try to show that you are

---

* Of course, not all popular people are snotty. Some people are popular and well-liked because they're genuine and friendly. But you know who I'm talking about—the ones who are popular but NOT well-liked, the ones who are condescending, the ones who pick and choose who they can talk to because of what clique they're in... The people who forget that we're all human, and think they're better than everyone else. If you can't stand someone's attitude, you can bet you're not the only one who notices and resents it. Just because someone appears to be "popular" (well-known) doesn't mean he or she is well-liked enough to win a majority of the votes.

just a "normal" person who wants to make a difference and work hard to help improve your school. Students would rather vote for someone who's really excited about doing the job than for someone who just wants another title to confirm for everyone how wonderful he or she is.

Even if the students you're running against are really good candidates—candidates even *you* would want to vote for—you just never know. It doesn't mean you can't beat them. They could split the majority of the votes and each have fewer votes than you. They could do something stupid and lose support. They could get overconfident and pompous, act like they've already won, and turn everyone off. They could give a really lame speech because they think they'll win anyway. They could get disqualified. They could drop out of the race. You never know what's going to happen.

Don't hold yourself back from running because you imagine someone else might do a better job than you. Come on, it's not brain surgery! Don't let your own self-doubt control you. Too often, the people you step out of the way for, letting them go ahead of you, end up disappointing you. They don't appreciate it, they forget, they lose enthusiasm, and they almost never do the job as well as you thought they would. You always end up kicking yourself for not going after something you wanted.

If you want the job, go for it! For everyone who wins, there's someone who doesn't. Nobody remembers, nobody cares. You cry a little and then move on. *The only real defeat is when you stop yourself from trying.* Then you're sure to lose.

Running can be fun, whether you win or not. (If you *make* it fun.) If you focus on the right things during your campaign, you can have a great time, earn respect from your classmates, and meet new people.

If you run a good race and make a good effort, you'll have a lot to be proud of, regardless of the outcome. Throwing yourself into the ring can do wonders for your confidence and self-esteem.

Also, your chances are far better than you'd think—especially if you're reading this book and learning from the successes and failures of others who have done what you're about to do.

If your school requires you to be nominated, and you want to run, go ahead and ask someone to nominate you. It's perfectly okay to ask someone to do this for you, because the voters will still make up their own minds. Don't lose the opportunity to run because you sat by silently and wished someone had thought of nominating you.

Be aware of the deadline. Decide to run, or decide not to run, but let it be your own deliberate choice—don't miss out because you were accidentally too late to sign up.

If the thing that's stopping you is FEAR (a four-letter word), please, just suck it up and take a deep breath. Picture how proud you'll be if you win; picture yourself running a good race and having fun with it; think of the friends you may not have met yet who you could have an excuse to talk to and meet during the campaign... Think of how young you are, and say to yourself, "If I don't attempt this now, when will I ever have the guts to—or the chance to?" And then *GO FOR IT!*

The popular students that run for an office already assume that they'll win, therefore they don't do as much. What I mean is that they don't go out of their way. The popular people are usually known by nearly everyone, but not necessarily liked by them all. The underdog knows this and is smart enough to go after voters, most of whose minds really aren't made up yet.

Tracee Lewis
President of Senate
Brandon, Florida

School kids aren't as dumb as some people would like to label them. Many students will really vote for the candidate that they actually think will do the most for the class, not just the person everyone expects to win because of popularity.

Kris Long
Class Vice-President
Davie, Florida

People who would be running against a popular opponent often forget that the "in" crowd probably makes up no more than 10% of the school (and therefore only 10% of the vote), and the rest are just the normal kids (90% of the vote).

Shawn A. Gaudette
Voter
Springfield, Massachusetts

Just an observation: if the votes are split among several candidates, an underdog can sneak in and win... With a class of 100, and 50% voting, someone can win with only 20 votes! (50 votes split 15-15-20)

Erik Wang
Voter
Lexington, Massachusetts

Many of us cannot stand the know-it-all people who get into office. They think they are better than anyone else and a lot of voters would love to see them beat by ANYBODY.

Heather Ann Kanski
Drama Club President
Richmond, Virginia

During my senior year, I ran for Class Treasurer against one of the you-can't-beat-me types (a cute blonde cheerleader). I had run for an office the year before, so everyone knew my name. She must have gotten scared that people would actually consider voting for me instead of her, because about 2 days before the voting was to take place, she dropped her name from the ballot, forfeiting the election. Persistence and sticking in there pays off.

Michelle Girton
Senior Class Treasurer
Levittown, Pennsylvania

Don't back down from an election just because the "popular" person is running. Most of the time, they're relying on their popularity to get them the job and don't have many new or good ideas to bring with them. If you do have the ideas, go for it. The "public" may support that popular person during their campaign, but when it comes down to the pencil and the ballot, most people go with the better choice, even if they lie about it later.

Katie Burnett
Voter
Naples, Florida

It is not what you do that you'll regret the most, it is the things you do not do. Half the school would like to run for an office, but is too afraid. You can't let fear stop you from doing what you really want to do. Fear is nothing. It has no smell, no taste, no feel, no sound, yet it is our biggest limitation. But fear will hold you back only if you allow it to. You can't let fear steal your dreams from you. If you want to run for election but you're afraid of losing, remember, if you lose, you will be in the same position you are in now, except you will not have to look back in twenty years and say "I wish I had run for an office." If giving a speech is what bothers you, ask yourself, "Am I going to let a sixty-second speech keep me from what I want?" Be the master of your own destiny. We don't control how long we live, but we certainly can control how much we do.

Jason Miller
Voter
Clovis, California

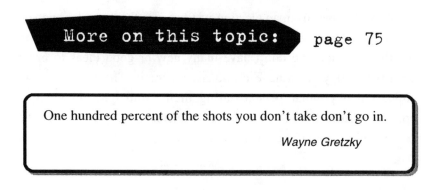

More on this topic: page 75

One hundred percent of the shots you don't take don't go in.

Wayne Gretzky

THE RIGHT ATTITUDE

The number one most important thing you need to win a high school election is *the right attitude.*

That doesn't mean "think positive, gray skies are gonna clear up, the sun'll come out tomorrow, look on the bright side and pretend everything's Marsha Brady"—it doesn't mean be fake-cheery and annoyingly-peppy—it means be the right kind of person.

Elections are not like blind computer-graded tests where everyone is treated equally. Students vote for who they *like,* not necessarily who they think is best-qualified. The students who you think are most "popular" may not necessarily be the best *liked.* If they're snotty and disliked, your class may in fact be happy to vote against them.

Everyone has natural enemies—you can't please everyone—but for the most part, your attitude about the election, and your attitude in general (the way you treat people) is the biggest reason your peers will want to vote for you or against you.

A humble, friendly, fun, positive attitude will make people like you and want to vote for you. On the other hand, a stuck-up and self-concerned attitude will create enemies and resentment, and definitely lose votes for you.

Keep in mind that an attitude is something you carry with you at all times. It will come through to everyone around you in your speech, your campaigning, and your posters. It is the kind of person you should choose to *be,* not something you can *act like.*

Be a friendly, approachable, nice, easy-to-be-around kind of person (the kind of person who smiles a lot and is genuinely glad to talk to everyone), and you'll have a much easier time getting people to support you.

Elections aren't about posters, they're about PEOPLE.

Smile. Talk to people. You don't have to already be "friends" with people to be *friendly* with them.

Don't look at campaigning as something you've "got" to do—look at it as something you "get" to do—use it as an opportunity to have some fun, and as a reason to push yourself to be a little more outgoing than usual.

The number one piece of advice repeated over and over and over by more than 1,000 students about how to win a high school election was this: **BE YOURSELF!**

DON'T turn into Mr. or Ms. Slick Willie at election time. Don't plastic-smile and kiss babies. Don't pretend you're perfect. Don't try to be someone you're not.

Be relaxed! Be friendly! Just talk to people!

Above all, be yourself. There's nothing more appealing than someone who is natural and who doesn't put up a false front.

Your classmates have to *want* to vote for you. They will *want* to vote for you if they *like* you. They will *like* you if you have a positive, easygoing, accessible, friendly, and genuine attitude.

Honestly, who would really vote for the prom queen when she won't give you the time of day? Relax and be yourself, promote your ideas, and be friendly to everyone. Have a very approachable attitude.

Lori MacEachern
Voter
Falmouth, Massachusetts

Be yourself—don't be fake, because people can ALWAYS pick up on it. It's annoying when candidates come around and pretend to be your friend just because they want your vote... Be real and you WILL be elected.

Melissa Lynn
Student Council Representative
Jackson, Michigan

Be sincere. Say things that YOU are really convicted about. Don't merely try to say what you think everyone else wants to hear. I can pick out phonies when they say things I've heard a thousand times before, or when their tone of voice sounds like they're reading off a speech their mommy wrote for them. When you are truly speaking from your heart about things you want to see happen and a difference you want to make, you will capture the voters' respect.

Jennifer Tiffan
Club President
Mesa, Arizona

Props and handouts and even a ton of posters don't matter. What does matter is meeting as many people as possible and remembering their names. Be personable. Shake hands. Give thanks to your supporters and volunteers in your campaign speech. Don't waste time listing your credentials. In most elections, all credentials are impeccable, and it just becomes a mess of organizations and awards no one remembers. What matters is the people.

Chad Silker
Student Body President
Rochester, Minnesota

Be nice to everyone. Most people don't even care who gets elected. But if people see your name on that voting slip and they think, "Hey, I remember that person, he/she was really nice," they will most likely check your name before the others.

Melissa Lewis
Voter
Philo, Ohio

Goals, platforms, etc. aren't very important. Let's face it, most of that stuff never comes true anyway and all the students know it. Instead, just try to be someone the students as a whole can relate to. People are much more apt to vote for friends than for politicians.

Josh Bean
Voter
Colorado Springs, Colorado

Real people get real votes. That is why the underdogs are sometimes able to win against the most popular kids in their schools. A relationship with the people and building the campaign from the roots up make all the difference.

Emiley L. Erb
Voter
Chesapeake, Virginia

Even if you are scared out of your wits, have an attitude of confidence—but not arrogance—people notice the difference.

Shannon Hinkle
Class President
Clarksville, Indiana

Don't say things like "When I am elected..." This tells people that you are too sure of yourself. You should say, "If I am elected..." This sounds a lot better, and it tells people that you hope to be elected, and that you're asking them to vote for you, not that you are already sure you'll win.

Travis S. Rice
Student Council Vice-President
Davie, Florida

More on this topic: page 83

Nothing astonishes men more than common sense and fair dealing.

Ralph Waldo Emerson

A GREAT SPEECH

Whether you like it or not, in most schools, students are going to make up their minds about who to vote for based almost entirely on the campaign speeches.

Your speech is totally under your control. You can make it long or short (make it short!). You can make it overly-serious or lighthearted (make it funny!). You can be stuffy and formal or you can talk like a normal person (be normal!). You can be scared stiff or you can be confident and relaxed (be in control!).

This is your opportunity to make a statement, to have it heard by a captive audience, and to deliver it with a big punch. This is your best chance to be funny, to be charming, to be confident, to be passionate, and to be sincere.

Your mission, if you choose to accept it, is to make an often intimidating endeavor (speaking before an audience) FUN.

Whatever you do, DON'T drone on and on. Keep it short. This is difficult to do, because there's a lot you want to say, and it's natural to want to repeat your important points again and again. Be aware that your peers have short attention spans and will tune-out if your speech gets boring or repetitive. The key is to *get in, get out, and sit down.* Voters appreciate it when you can say what you have to say confidently and succinctly and not waste their time.

Do NOT plan to just get up and improvise. Prepare! It may feel stupid to practice your speech beforehand, but preparation is the key to conquering nerves. Having gone through your speech several times—out loud, in front of people—will make you much more confident and less nervous in front of your classmates.

Public speaking is the number one fear admitted by most people. If you think about it too much, you can easily psyche yourself out and think everyone's looking at you, they're going to laugh at you, you're going to be put on the spot, etc.

You can't let it get you! Take control! You talk to your classmates all the time, in lunch, in class, after school, etc. The only difference here is that they're actually captive and quiet. This is your big chance to make an impression.

You can totally surprise and disarm them by *not* being nervous. Talk to them like you always do, with sincerity, strength and ease, and you'll give off the sense that you're a natural born leader.

Getting started is the hardest part. If you're nervous, you have to think about what you're trying to say and *pretend* you're sure of yourself. Once you get going, you won't have to pretend anymore, because the momentum will give you real confidence.

If you're not nervous, something's wrong. Everybody naturally gets the adrenaline pumping when they're about to do something they care about.

But don't let fear debilitate you! After all, what's fear? It's all in your head. You can use the excitement to focus your energy on being down-to-earth and cutting through the usual formality of campaign speeches in order to *communicate,* or you can let your knees shake and worry about how your hair looks.

If you look at the speech as your big chance (probably your only chance) to show everyone your fun, lighthearted attitude and persuade them that you want to work hard for the class, then you can, in a short and simple speech, *right then and there*, get all the votes you need to win the election.

Go for broke. Make it or break it.

Your peers do NOT want you to mess up. Really, most of them don't even care. Half of them will be either sleeping, staring at the clock, or thinking about the weekend.

Even if you see them all sitting there facing you, it's pretty safe to assume that most of their minds are elsewhere. You've got to capture their attention and get your point across in a way that they'll *want* to respond to.

Making a campaign speech is a lot like telling a joke. Nobody's hanging on your every word. You have to make it interesting. It can't be too long, it can't be dull like a weather report, and it can't be too serious. You can't *force* them to pay attention; you have to make them *want* to listen.

Usually, that means that funny speeches win elections.

Don't start your speech with a standard "insert joke here" joke, say or do something funny that is *you,* something that implies "I'm here because I *want* to be here, I voluntarily *choose* to be here doing this, and I'm going to try to make this fun."

Don't read your speech like a book report. It's not being graded. Just *talk* to your peers about something you're asking them to do—vote. Tell them why. Use your passion to persuade them, *from one student to another,* that you would be a great candidate to elect.

You have to *ask* them to vote for you. Not *tell* them—*ask* them.

You already know there's a tremendous difference between talking "at" someone (lecturing) and talking "with" them (discussing). When you're in front of an audience, of course, they're not talking back (we hope), so you can't actually talk "with" them. However, your tone of voice, your manner, and your ATTITUDE should indicate that you're just a normal student who has something valuable to say.

Try to make the listeners feel comfortable. Make them laugh. Don't get all formal. Don't act above them or talk down to them. Just be "one of them," saying why you want to volunteer for the job of working hard *for them.* Tell them why winning the election is important to you and why representing them is something you'll be proud to do.

If you honestly mean it, it will show.

You can't let a school election be life-or-death to you, but you can still be passionate about it. If you're going to bother doing it at all, do it with *zest.* You want to come across in your speech as prepared and confident, but also as easy-going and fun.

Remember, the most important thing is your attitude. Be confident and humble and friendly and genuine. Whatever you do, *BE YOURSELF.*

Have the mindset that you're there to *share,* not lecture. Do you remember doing "show-and-tell" in first grade? Were you nervous? Of course not, you were too busy concentrating on the frog you brought in, and what you wanted to *share* about it. You were talking enthusiastically about something you were excited about, and you were trying to make everyone else as interested in it as you were. Try to recapture that informal, non-presentational feeling of "show-and-tell."

Your speech does not have to conform to the mood set by the others that come before and after it. Just because everyone else is scared and straight-laced doesn't mean you have to be. Let them do their thing. Do your own.

The one that stands out is usually the only one remembered.

Your opponents will probably get up and go on and on about why they're so wonderful. They'll list everything impressive they've ever done, implying that the audience should add it all up and see how terrific they are. Well, guess what—nobody cares! Don't make your whole speech about *me*, make it about *we*. Make it about next year and what you want to do for the class. Be specific.

Anybody with enthusiasm for the job can be a great class officer. *What you plan to do is far more important than what you have done.*

Get people to help you prepare your speech. If, as a class officer, you're really going to get the class involved and be a great leader, why not start now and get a few of your friends to help you make a great speech? It's not cheating, it's being smart!

If your school allows it, you could even get someone popular or funny to say a few words about you and introduce you. There's no reason you can't have other students endorsing you as a candidate, holding signs or other visual aids for you, rapping behind you as your "boom-box," or even escorting you up to the podium and cheering for you. Get creative.

Don't let the prospect of giving a speech scare you. It's something you should get excited about! Don't think of it as a dead-serious plea for votes (like a PBS pledge-drive), think of it more as a *skit,* a chance to have some fun, to cause a few laughs, and to share your enthusiasm.

You can make it a drag, or you can make it fun and clever and mischievous and dynamic. You can make it long and boring, or you can make it exciting and cool. You can make it blend in with all the others, or you can make it surprising and funny and memorable.

Again: *funny speeches usually win high school elections.*

The best speeches were those that made the class laugh. And they were short. Long, boring speeches never won.

> Erin McLaughlin
> Voter
> Savannah, Georgia

The campaign speech is where most people decide whether the candidate is genuine or just trying to win them over. The person running must demonstrate that the students, and what the candidate wants to do for them, are far more important to him/her than just winning.

> Ashlyn Caysee Agler
> Student Council President
> Detroit, Michigan

Have your speech planned out. Don't go up there fumbling for words. Don't expect to have the answers off the top of your head. Actually plan out what you want to get accomplished and then present it clearly and quickly.

> Kaycie Newman
> Student Council President
> Chicago, Illinois

There were always people who would get up without a prepared speech, and just say something like, "I'm not going to make one of those stupid speeches telling you why I should be elected... you guys know who the best president should be." Those people always seemed to me to be the most moronic idiots. If they couldn't even take the time to prepare a two minute speech, do you think they will prepare themselves enough to run the entire student body?? It is a dire mistake to take that approach, in my opinion.

> Jennifer Brown
> Voter
> Oxnard, California

Whoever invented the phrase "try to picture the audience in their underwear" was an idiot. The way to be confident in a campaign speech is to just know what you're trying to say, so it won't matter if you mess up. If you're comfortable with what you're saying and believe in it, it will show.

Kathryn Bertram
Student Council President
Columbus, Ohio

Use your hands. Wave them if you want, fix your hair while you talk if you want, just don't put them down by your side or on the front of the podium and let them stay there. It IS ok to say uhh and umm, just not every other word. Think about what you're saying, it makes the whole thing more interesting. Smile, use different facial expressions and voice tones. Most of all, just be yourself, because you are far from boring.

Joshua Clements
Voter
Mount Holly, North Carolina

I don't know why people put their entire speeches on notecards. That just feeds into the "this is how one is SUPPOSED to address a crowd" mentality. Same thing with staring at a spot on the wall over people's heads. Oh, please! If you are trying to communicate, then you should speak right to the people, with only a page or two of notes to keep you on track so you don't have to worry about leaving something out. If you relax, it'll give the audience permission to relax too.

Nick Finsterwald
Class Vice-President
Buffalo, New York

One way that people consistently persuade others toward their views is if they have a passion for what they are talking about. It's the simple difference of talking from your head or talking from your heart. You can't make people believe in something if you do not believe in it yourself.

> *Michael A. Ganiere*
> *Junior Class President*
> *Milwaukee, Wisconsin*

When a person is really confident and gets in front of a group and is totally comfortable, people notice that. It is sort of like vibes emanate from the person and the audience catches those vibes. They tell the audience the speaker is true to what she's saying and really believes in herself.

> *Nickole Rucker*
> *Class President*
> *Denver, Colorado*

Even if you are scared to death to be in front of people, if you do a good enough job of pretending that you're not, no one will know the difference. Confidence is everything.

> *Jason D. Sopko*
> *Senior Class President*
> *Parma Heights, Ohio*

People don't want to hear your past achievements or stuff like that, they want to hear about who you are and what you can do for them.

> *Greg Nunn*
> *Voter*
> *Mulvane, Kansas*

High school students can't go ranting and raving about how they will do things to make the school a better place, like eliminating homework... That's not realistic. People running for election should try to make people see things as they really are, and focus on one goal they will try to accomplish if and when they are elected.

Elizabeth Foraker
Voter
Cleveland, Ohio

The main key to winning a high school election is humor—making funny speeches and hanging up funny posters. Nobody wants to hear campaign jibber. You know all the other candidates will be dry and serious.

Amanda Ross
Voter
Lexington, Kentucky

Make the audience laugh, don't bore them. They'll remember something funny more than the same old thing everyone says.

Molly Atwood
Voter
Columbus, Ohio

A girl named Laura who ran for Vice President began giving a usual "elect me" speech, but then, all of the sudden stopped, and said, "I can't do this anymore. You know, when I told my little brother that I was nervous about giving my speech, he told me to picture the audience in their underwear. Hey, look!" Then she pointed to the back of the auditorium. A friend of hers (who happened to be a guy) had snuck into the back of the auditorium. He stood in the spotlight with only his boxer shorts on. The crowd was hysterical! By the time they looked back at the podium for Laura, she had disappeared, but a sign that said "Vote for Laura Baldwin" was in her place. That was by far the most clever speech I had ever seen.

Amy Kowalski
Voter
Westfield, Massachusetts

I had a friend named Will who was running for Vice-President of the Senior class, and when he did his speech he was wearing a button down shirt and slacks. While he was talking about the qualities and things you need in a Vice-President, he was slowly unbuttoning his shirt. Finally, he said, "But the most important thing you need is WILL POWER!!" And by then, his shirt was completely unbuttoned and pulled off to show a red T-shirt underneath with WILL POWER put on it with those fuzzy iron-on letters. Needless to say, he won the election by a landslide for his sense of fun and his charisma.

Leslie Brown
Voter
Houston, Texas

"I'd like to ask everyone to please move all the way over to the left side of your seats. Now move all the way to the right. Now everyone turn around and introduce yourself to the person behind you, and to the people on your left and right. Now, if I can clean the seats and introduce you to at least one new person in as little as five minutes, then think of what I can do in an entire year." This was part of a speech used at my high school last year by a girl who won by a landslide.

Monica Buckley
Student Council Vice-President
Dallas, North Carolina

More on this topic: page 102

More ideas for speeches: page 49

If you want to get an audience with you, there's only one way. You have to reach out to them with total honesty and humility.

Frank Sinatra

TALK TO PEOPLE AND ASK THEM TO VOTE

A lot of times, when students go into the voting booth, they don't really know the candidates or remember any of the platforms. All the campaigning just blends together into a blur, and they vote for the only person they remember, or the only name they recognize.

Usually, nobody but the candidates themselves really cares very much about the outcome of the election or thinks about the school's "issues" as much as the candidates wish they would.

So it really doesn't take all that much to get votes.

All you need is for students to, first, *remember* you; second, remember but *not dislike* you; and third, go to the polls and *vote*. It's that simple.

People will remember and consider how you acted towards them personally far more than they'll care about your speech, your posters, your platform, or anything else. Don't underestimate the power of meeting and talking to people on a one-on-one basis.

In the voting booth, people will, for the most part, think about whether you were nice or snotty to them; whether your campaign was good and heartfelt, lackluster, or annoying; and whether they think you're going to be a good representative for the class or just someone on a personal power-trip.

It may not be fair, but such is life.

Don't make the mistake of thinking people are going to necessarily vote based on the criteria they *should*. Don't assume anyone will necessarily vote for the best candidate. Don't assume anyone even knows or cares who is the best candidate.

People usually vote for their friends—it's true. But not necessarily their *old* friends. High school students usually vote for the candidate they liked best *during the campaign.*

Sure, best friends always vote for their best friends, and small cliques usually support the members of their own clique. But probably 80% of the voters are up for grabs. Most of them (if they vote at all) will think about what they've seen in the campaign and then vote for the person who left them with the best impression—often, the only candidate who took the time to talk to them personally and ask them to vote.

Picture this scenario: you're walking down the hall, and you see two candidates. One is busy hanging posters, the other is hanging around with the students and chatting. The first one sees you but turns his/her back to you (he/she must think the posters are more important than the students), the other smiles and introduces him/herself, gives you a sticker, and asks you to please remember to vote. Which one would you prefer to support? Which one do you think will do a better job of representing the students?

How about this: you're in an elevator with two other students. One stares at his book or at the floor and pretends you're not there, the other simply says "hi." That's it. The elevator stops and you go your separate ways. You don't really give it much thought, but everything else being equal, which person do you *like* more? Which one would you rather see win?

It's tiny little interactions like these that get you votes. Believe it or not.

Remember, you don't have to get *all* the votes. It doesn't have to be unanimous. You just have to get one more vote than each one of your competitors. The more candidates you're running against (the more chances there are to split the votes), the fewer votes you need.

Even if the vast majority of the votes go to your opponents—for example, out of 100 votes, if two of your opponents each get 33 votes ($\frac{2}{3}$ of the votes are NOT for you) and you get 34 votes (only just slightly over $\frac{1}{3}$ of the votes)—who wins?

Winning by one vote is as good as winning by a hundred.

Every vote you can get is important.

Remember, *not everyone votes!* The winning candidate is often simply the one who got the most people to go cast ballots!

People who you've encouraged to go vote will usually vote for you. You don't even have to say "vote for me." If you ask people merely to "please be sure to vote" or "please remember to make a choice" instead of saying "vote for me," it sounds better. It's more humble. It's more socially acceptable. Of course *they know* that you want them to vote only for you. But if you focus on the best interest of the class (letting the voters choose the best candidate) instead of selfishly promoting yourself, more students will respond to your request (cast a vote), and they'll most likely vote for you anyway because they appreciate your attitude.

Don't assume people will vote. You should *ask* them to.

If it's true at your school that most people don't care about elections, then this apathy is your biggest obstacle *and* your best friend. You'll be way ahead of the competition if you can put yourself in the shoes of a voter and realize that students need a *reason* to vote for you. The fact that they *like you and want to support you* is the easiest and most effective reason.

The best candidate doesn't always win! The one who campaigns the best (without being fake) and who gets the most people to vote does.

If you recognize that every single individual vote you can get is important, and you concentrate your energies on getting *individual people* to vote for you, you'll have a tremendous advantage over the candidates who think in terms of mass-marketing and believe that slick posters alone will turn into "everyone" voting for them.

In the voting booth, there is no "everyone," there are only individuals.

Use the campaign as an excuse to be friendly and talk to people. Let your classmates know that you're running and that you want to help improve the school. Push yourself to say hello to people and initiate conversations—in hallways, in elevators, in cafeteria lunch lines—anywhere and anytime you can. Running for election gives you something to talk about. It gives you a *reason*, an *excuse* to talk to people you usually don't get to.

They *know* you want something from them. You don't have to hit them over the head with it. Just relax and be friendly.

Don't turn your back to students in the hallways and hang more posters; hang around in the hallways and talk to more students!

It's all about people. Everything else is secondary.

Be a real person and not just a name. Get your face noticed around the school and you will be amazed at what happens!!!

Jessica Dolinsky
Voter
Scranton, Pennsylvania

Before I sustained a severe head injury and memory loss as the result of a motorcycle accident, I had never really taken the time to meet people. But one would be surprised how much more pleasant life is when you decide to smile, loosen up, and make an effort to meet people. Even just a simple "hello" as you pass is a start. It is amazing how many people will smile back and reply "hi." Before long, you'll end up seeing and talking to so many people every day just because you said "hello" to them one time and they feel they know you. It's totally within your control: a simple change in your attitude and a willingness to meet people. And, of course, people vote for who they know. The more people you know, the better off you will be come election day.

Jason Miller
Voter
Clovis, California

Your typical popular girl who had been our Class President the previous year was running against a jock who no one expected to win. But the jock was the one who made the effort to talk to everyone, not only the "popular" kids. He was sincere in his actions and it led to a victory. Be genuinely friendly. Not the fake-smile friendly, but taking the time to hear everyone's thoughts and opinions. People who already think they will win don't always necessarily take advantage of this and often lose because of it.

Mel Mack
Voter
Wilbraham, Massachusetts

I think there is nothing more annoying than a person who is your BEST FRIEND once it comes to election time, and hates you for the rest of the year. Be open to ALL ideas. If you are running for class president and you think someone is a nerd or something, it DOESN'T matter. You are trying to represent the WHOLE class, INCLUDING nerds.

Ginger Joseph
Voter
Monument, Colorado

My downfall the first time I ran was that during campaign time, I didn't talk to people. I should've walked up to people and talked to them instead of being so secluded and hard to find. The candidate who won, even though his speech was bad, had spent time getting to know people, talking to people, asking people what they thought needed to be changed in the way the student body was run. Had I done that, I think I would've gotten that one extra vote I needed to win.

Nickole Rucker
Class President
Denver, Colorado

The classic way for an underdog to win an election: go for the votes that others wouldn't think about. I had a friend who was not popular, but who actually went out and campaigned. He went from clique to clique, introducing himself and asking people what they wanted in the student government. He went around and talked to people and listened to them. The students responded, voting the team captain out.

Nick Tramontin
Voter
Los Angeles, California

The most important thing I'd tell people running for office is to get out the vote. I had a majority of people's support... I just didn't get them down to the foyer to vote.

> *Robert Smuts*
> *Voter*
> *Sharon, Massachusetts*

Most of the students don't care who wins the election. Really, it only matters to the candidates. It is sad, but at that level (high school students), the population just doesn't care. I think one of the most important things for a candidate to do is not be afraid to put themselves on the line. If, a day or two before the election, you remind students that you would appreciate their vote, it will go a long way. Candidates at the high school level should not be afraid to ask for a vote. Because most of their peers don't care, it will be easy to convince them (as long as you're on good terms).

> *Daniel Steigerwalt*
> *President, National Honor Society*
> *East Stroudsburg, Pennsylvania*

Encourage everyone to register WITHOUT mentioning your campaign at all. Let people know that winning is not the only thing on your mind.

> *Joshua Karns*
> *Student Council President*
> *Camp Hill, Pennsylvania*

As long as you can get people who most likely wouldn't be voting anyway, to vote at all, they will probably vote for you.

> *Jeremy Myrland*
> *Student Council Treasurer*
> *Dallas, Oregon*

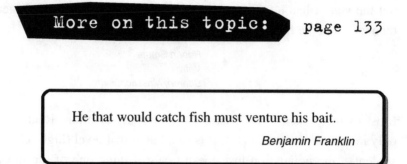

More on this topic: page 133

He that would catch fish must venture his bait.

Benjamin Franklin

GETTING YOUR NAME REMEMBERED

POSTERS

Posters alone do not win elections.

It's not an art contest. Nobody really pays much attention to posters, especially if there are a lot of them competing for attention. Your posters should be colorful, simple, and cleverly placed in unique high-traffic spots. Something about them should stand out and make people notice your name.

Your name should be the biggest and boldest thing on the poster. If someone glances at the poster for just one second (which is all—or more—than many students will), what's the one thing you want him or her to clearly notice and remember? *Your name.*

Don't overdo it with the posters. You get no points for how artistic or intricate they are. You don't get votes by having the most or the biggest posters. All posters can do is remind people that you want the job, that you're promising to do the job well, that you've got a cool attitude about the election, and that you're asking them to vote for you.

Remember what posters are for, and don't get sidetracked into thinking they *are* the campaign. They're just reminders.

Reminders of what? That's the important part. Concentrate on campaigning (introducing yourself to people on a personal, individual basis and asking them to vote), and your great speech, and don't worry so much about fancy posters.

The person who is the most visible is often the one elected. When you get a ballot, you will automatically ignore any names you don't know, and vote for the one you have heard the most about.

> *Toni McQuilken*
> *Voter*
> *Oviedo, Florida*

The biggest key for someone wanting to run for anything is of course having the majority of people know who you are somehow. In schools that are so big it is almost impossible for everyone to know everyone, you have to find some way to get your name out there.

> *Emily Haverkamp*
> *Voter*
> *Overland Park, Kansas*

Campaigning with posters develops an image for the candidate, but will not win an election. No one stops to read details on a poster, so it should simply state a point, your name, and something attention-catching.

> *Robert O'Brien*
> *Senior Council Senator*
> *Portland, Maine*

Put as few words as possible on your posters. When students are walking from class to class, they don't want to have to stop and read a big old long thing. They want to just get the necessary information and move on. It also makes a lot more impact if you can put your picture on your posters.

Laura Marshburn
School Spirit Commissioner
Palo Alto, California

They were doing construction at my school, putting up a new building. A guy running for President of the class had pictures blown up of himself in front of the construction site, smiling, wearing a hard hat, and holding a shovel. Underneath, he had his name and the caption, "Working hard to build a better school..."

Louis Ormin
Voter
Santa Barbara, California

One sign had a large picture of me in front of the TV at my house wearing pajamas. The caption read "Kyle Rossi last Saturday night." Across the top, in larger letters, it said, "People with nothing to do in their free time have lots of opportunities to work hard for the betterment of Solon High School." It went over so well that it spawned an entire series of similar signs.

Kyle Rossi
Class Treasurer
Solon, Ohio

More on this topic: page 145

More ideas for posters: page 65

HANDOUTS

A lot of candidates hand things out in the hallways and around the school: pamphlets, flyers, stickers, buttons, pencils, candy, etc.

This can be great publicity, but it could also work against you.

Be careful.

Nobody likes to be bribed.

Everybody wants to get something for nothing, but nobody wants to vote for someone who's trying to "buy" the election.

Handing things out—short letters addressed to the voters asking them to vote, platform summaries, surveys and requests for suggestions, or balloons/buttons/stickers with your name and a cute slogan on them—is usually a good thing. It can be a great way to get your name exposed, especially if you give out something that people will hold onto or wear or use or play with all day.

Having something to hand out can also make it easier for you to stop your classmates, meet them, and talk to them. But you're missing the point if you just thrust things at people and say "here, vote for me" like a robot. You don't want to make the handouts seem more important than the candidate. Instead, *use* handouts as a way to break the ice, an excuse to stop people and talk to them.

Remember, it's not about how many things you give out. It's about how people remember you as a candidate, and whether or not they even go vote at all. You want to ask them to vote and remind them to vote, NOT bribe them to vote.

A special note about giving out candy: popular opinion seems to be very divided on this. Some students swear by it, saying students will vote for whoever gives them the best snack. But others will think it's sleazy and desperate—even if it's *not* intended that way.

To give out candy or not to give out candy—that is the question. It comes down to a personal philosophy, what your competitors are doing, and what is customary in your school. You don't want to lose the election because your competitor gave out candy and you didn't—but on the other hand, you don't ever want to be thought of as someone who won the election *because* of the candy.

This is a strategic decision. You should consider the atmosphere in your school and what has been done before (what is expected). Is handing out candy common campaigning practice? Are others doing it? Could it hurt? Could it hurt your chances if you don't? Do you need it? Can it backfire? Could it get you disqualified?

My advice: rise above it. You can win without passing out candy.

But I don't know your school.

Think carefully about this decision. Don't blow it off. Ask your friends for advice. Which of the students below sounds most like your classmates (the ones who vote)?

Whatever you do, *don't* let your campaigning become "about" candy or stickers or whatever. Let your handouts, if you have any, serve as an introduction and an ice-breaker, *not as a platform.*

The best way to get people to know you is through campaigning. Especially posters and those stickers that people wear. Bribery may have worked in grade school, but high school students see right through that and basically think of it as desperate.

> *Mary Kelly*
> *Senior Class Treasurer*
> *Wilmington, Delaware*

The people who have always won are those that have their slogans not only on posters hanging up, but have a handout along with it. These constantly remind people who is running, and they usually explain that the candidate wants to win because he or she wants to serve the school.

> *Marisa Ruth Werner*
> *Voter*
> *West Valley City, Utah*

I went to Wal-Mart and bought florescent copy paper and a greeting card. Why a greeting card? Because I wrote my personal message to the students inside the greeting card, to the effect of, "Thank you for considering me as your Senior Reporter," and then I made 300 copies of that greeting card onto my fluorescent paper. I folded them all and handed them out with miniature candy bars stapled in the corner. Many people respected me for using a humble approach—asking them instead of commanding them to vote for me.

> *Briana Blount*
> *Senior Class Reporter*
> *Denham Springs, Louisiana*

Something that one candidate did, which I thought was pretty clever, was give out candy to everyone in the school—but attached to it was a picture of him, his slogan, and when and where the voting was taking place. It made him noticed throughout the student body and put a face with the name.

Jessica Dolinsky
Voter
Scranton, Pennsylvania

We tied the first time, with the exact same number of votes. It had never happened before in the history of my school, and no one knew what to do about it. They decided the only fair thing to do was have a re-election. We were not going to give another speech. Campaigning was the only thing we could do. So I went to an Office Depot and bought 1,300 pencils. I made little tags that said "I need your support. Vote Brooke President" and taped each tag to a pencil, and had them delivered to every homeroom the morning of the re-election. Four hours later, I found out I was the new Student Body President. People still tell me the pencils won my election.

Brooke Thompson
Student Body President
Clover, South Carolina

People who passed out stickers to wear or candy with their name on it had a better chance because when people went in to vote, if they didn't really know the people running (or didn't care), they would just look on their sticker or at the piece of candy they were eating and vote for the name on it. No joke.

Nicole Tobin
Student Council member
Livonia, Michigan

A lot of people in school elections give out candy. They may think it works, but bribery doesn't really work. The majority of students will vote for the person they think deserves the job and can do it well (otherwise they are someone who just votes for their friends anyway).

Melissa Gosdzinski
Voter
Southfield, Michigan

A great majority of students pass around small pieces of paper with their slogans on it and small pieces of candy, but this rarely works. People promise their vote to the candidate with candy, but will still vote for their friends.

Natalia Hermosillo
Drama Club Treasurer
El Paso, Texas

Don't give away stuff. It will make some people feel that you're trying to "buy" them (even if you're not), and most of them will take your gift and vote however they want anyway.

Bwana Hansen
Voter
St. Petersburg, Florida

Bribes don't work. Most people see bribery as an effort, by a loser, to make friends. People will take bribes and then laugh because they suckered the candidate.

Shaun G. Moe
Student Body President
Lakewood, Colorado

One candidate passed out lollipops with "Vote for Kevin" stickers on the bottom. Some people found them cute and others found them obnoxious. However, one of the opposing candidates hung a large wall-size poster which read, "Don't Be A Sucker... Vote for SUSIE."

Lori DelliColli
Class Vice-President
Methuen, Massachusetts

A person giving out candy usually seems to be using it as a bribe, maybe because he or she can't influence votes any other way... I don't know about you, but I look down on people that have to resort to bribing people for their votes...

Todd Stewart
Voter
Tampa, Florida

More on this topic: page 151

The advertisement is the most truthful part of a newspaper.

Thomas Jefferson

PART 2

IDEAS FOR SPEECHES AND POSTERS

IDEAS FOR SPEECHES

For speeches, don't be afraid to be creative. Dumb things are remembered. People have to sit through an hour of speeches, so make yours stand out. I've seen everything from people wearing their team uniform during speeches to stepping off the stage to "put themselves on everyone else's level."

Jessica Eule
Vice President of Senior Class
Parsippany, New Jersey

It's important to set yourself apart somehow, otherwise all the speeches just sound the same. Last year, the guy that won promised that he would turn our gym into a WCW wrestling ring and have wrestling every Friday, and we could all have the chance to powerbomb our principal. It was damn funny.

Jamie Messer
President, National Honor Society
Burlington, Iowa

In 8th grade, a guy who nobody really knew got up and gave the funniest speech. The joke was—because it was a year when both a teacher and the founder of the school had died—"As Treasurer, I'd like to see us spend some of our class's money to build a memorial tribute for Mrs. Schultz and Dr. MacMillan and all the other teachers who died this year." It was the blatant lack of respect in his deadpan delivery that made it so hilarious. The whole room was cracking up (even the teachers in the room), and he won by a landslide.

Mindy Walker
Voter
Fort Lauderdale, Florida

The things that really influenced me were the people that just had fun with their speeches. One kid won with a campaign promise of quilted toilet paper for a week in the bathrooms. Another guy quoted and then interpreted the unintelligible words of some obscure WWF friend of his. What counts is that you have fun, because if you're not having fun, you can bet they won't be either.

Dan Lash
Voter
Overland Park, Kansas

Something that a guy at my high school promised to do if he was elected—our locker rooms smelled pretty bad, so he promised to get rid of the "pee" smell that invaded our locker rooms. I think that is what got him elected.

Tara Howard
Voter
Riverbank, California

If your school has a uniform, a good idea would be to fight for a relaxed dress code... if not a permanent one, maybe twice a month so the school doesn't feel like a jail.... the person who did this won.

> *J.R. Kennie*
> *Student Senate Representative*
> *River Forest, Illinois*

I had a friend who ran for office in band and one of her goals was to clean off the teacher's desk. Everyone laughed at that and voted for her.

> *Crystal Crowell*
> *Voter*
> *Whitehall, Ohio*

One idea is to offer a Student Council sponsored "Clean Our Highways" day. I proposed this to the students during my speech and they bought it. We ended up with 200 out of a Senior class of 1000 cleaning the road one Saturday morning. We got our pictures in the paper and everything...

> *G. Jeffrey O'Malley*
> *Student Council Representative*
> *Frankfort, Illinois*

Our Senior Class President was elected because she promised to bring back the Senior Trip. She gave out fliers for a trip to Mazatlan, Mexico, and was elected the next second. She successfully appealed to the majority of the Seniors, because who could turn down a 300 dollar trip to Mexico for a week with no chaperones?

> *Amanda Terrill*
> *Voter*
> *Phoenix, Arizona*

One brave kid at my school won the election for school president on the platform of putting a pencil sharpener in every room. It takes a lot of guts to stand up in front of the school and say something that may sound that stupid, but it shows that you're not afraid to look dumb, and that you really want to do something worthwhile for the school. (If you don't need pencil sharpeners in your school, substitute something else that should be commonplace, but isn't.)

Evan Lewis
Voter
Scarsdale, New York

A girl who was running for president of our Sophomore class put a big emphasis on making sure the bathrooms are clean and have doors on every stall, and good stuff like that. It drew a huge response from my friends (mostly the football players), with lots of hoots and hollering, and she left to a bigger standing ovation than any of the other candidates (even the football players and cheerleaders who were running). She ended up winning the election. This shows the importance of some issues to people, no matter how outrageous, and, I guess, also shows that anyone can win.

Kevin Gogan
Voter
Bloomington, Minnesota

Some students running for Class Representative are just kidding around. They go on stage and say, "Well, girls and boys, last year the toilet paper was way too hard. Let's fight together, all fight for a better world, fight for softer toilet paper!" And it works! I have to confess that we don't really take these elections very seriously because we all know these Class Representatives are not very powerful and can't really change much. Anybody who's really crazy or funny gets elected!

Beatrice Flaig
Voter
Lower Saxony, Germany

I saw this guy give a speech. He wasn't the smallest guy in the world—okay let's get down to it, he was "husky," "chunky," whatever you want to call it, he was fat. My favorite part of his speech was, "Remember, there is more of me to work for you." I thought that was awesome, because he was joking around and not taking himself too seriously...

Bart Edwards
Voter
San Diego, California

One fellow running for Secretary of the Student Government stood behind the podium and read a fairly bizarre but extremely articulate speech, without looking at the audience once. One of his suggestions was that we change the school's mascot to an iguana—he made positive analogies and comparisons of iguanas and their abilities and behaviors and such to the student-body. He so impressed the student-body with his mad but entertaining genius that they elected him.

Joe Kaufman
Voter
Scarsdale, New York

One guy who was elected President when I was a Junior dressed up as Forrest Gump and began his speech, "My name is Matt Brass, and I'm running for President. Would you like a chocolate? Mama always said..." You know the rest. Even though he had everyone laughing hysterically, at the end of his speech he got serious and said that he loved our school and the student body. He got the attention of the crowd, but then he also showed that he wasn't in it just for fun and games.

Leanne Suber
Voter
Newnan, Georgia

One great line from a campaign speech (spoken very clearly, with each syllable of his name spoken one at a time, slowly): "My name is Jack Stahlman. Take a good look at me." He then proceeded to turn sideways to give us all a good look at his mugshot. It was a riot. He won by a landslide.

Chad Silker
Student Body President
Rochester, Minnesota

One of the guys running for Student Body President gave a spectacular speech. It had very little to do with platform or goals or anything, it just made us laugh. He started talking about the old TV show "Saved By the Bell" and of course everyone had seen the show, knew all the characters, etc. The funny thing was, no would have admitted to watching that show. But he knew that even though we were cool about it in the halls, that we really had seen the show, and he used it to give a very funny speech. I don't even remember how it related to the rest of his speech, but he basically told about one episode in which Zach, Kelly, Screech, Slater, Jessie, and Lisa were all trying to save the Max because the school board wanted to turn it into a parking lot. As it turns out, almost everyone had seen that exact same episode! At first we were all reluctant to admit it, because it was kind of a dorky show, but it put us all on the same level. By bringing up this subject that we (even as Freshmen) acted "too cool for," he made himself seem very real. He wasn't some bloated cocky jerk like some of the other candidates, he was just one of us. By making himself just another student, we were all more apt to vote for him because he would know how to represent the average student. It worked, and he was elected President.

Josh Bean
Voter
Colorado Springs, Colorado

One guy delivered such a funny speech that he won, hands down, because of it. He was Asian, and his speech was something to the effect of, "When I was a little boy growing up in Korea, my mother was very ill. She took me to her bedside and said, 'Son, I am dying and I have one last wish for you. You must become SGA President.' So I must now honor my mother's wish and serve as President. If you do not vote for me, you will be betraying my mother's last wish." It really was very funny.

Nicole Steinmetz
Voter
McLean, Virginia

My speech went something like this (or at least the funny part): "I come from a family where both my parents are accountants. So I hear my father say (in father-like demanding voice), 'Son, be an accountant,' and I hear my mother say (in high pitched, fast voice), 'You know, dear, I'll support you in whatever you do, but I'd really appreciate it if you'd be an accountant.' So, I decided to run for Treasurer and fulfill some of my parents wishes. Today, I ask you to help me in that effort."

Kenneth G. Pittman
State Mu Alpha Theta Treasurer
Knoxville, Tennessee

A guy running for Secretary started his speech by announcing that he was dropping out of the race. Then, over the speakers, came a pre-recorded tape of what was supposed to be the voice of God (really, his voice), telling him not to be a fool, and to stay in the race. It was really funny and people remembered it and he won.

Laura Marshburn
School Spirit Commissioner
Palo Alto, California

A guy who ran for A.S.B. President my Junior year played the Superman music in the background while he read his speech. He started mentioning the traits that he felt he had in common with Superman and, at the climax of the music and his speech, he ripped open his shirt and underneath was a Superman shirt. He won, and I think it was because he used something that the students really felt they could relate to and enjoy, not to mention that it was very memorable.

> *Jennifer L. Stair*
> *Voter*
> *Kennewick, Washington*

"Okay, everyone stand up. Now move one step to your left. Now move one step to your right. Now sit down. Thank you. My father said that I would win if I could move the crowd."

> *Maynard James Keenan*
> *Middle School President*
> *Bedford, Massachusetts*

The best and most amusing campaign speech I ever saw went like this: the candidate got up to make his speech. He said he had a little demonstration to show us. He hit a tape player and then began STRIPPING! First his belt, then his shirt and pants. With these off, he stood there in gym shorts and a Student Council Shirt. He stopped the music. He looked at his watch and said, "If I can make this sort of change in fifteen seconds, think what I could do with a whole school year." The audience whooped and hollered and was going nuts. He simply walked off stage after that and won the Senior Class Vice-Presidency by a landslide. Everyone else droned on for ten minutes, and I remember nothing from their speeches, but I will remember the "strip show" forever.

> *Sarah Oltvedt*
> *Voter*
> *Kansas City, Missouri*

For my speech, I did a take-off of David Letterman's Top 10 List. I did the top 10 reasons to vote for me, and I used certain inside jokes that only the students would understand, like certain rules and incidents that happened. Well, it worked and I won! Always put a little of yourself and your personality in your speeches and your campaign. No one wants to vote for the "same ol' Joe." You have to give people a little bit of flavor.

Erin June
Homecoming Queen
Tampa, Florida

Here are a few things that I've witnessed: wearing a full chicken suit when giving the campaign speech; choosing a random TV character as one's campaign "mascot" and putting this character on all of the posters. (My friend used Mr. Drummond and Arnold from Different Strokes, and made little hand held signs with their heads on them for people to wave while he was making his speech); wearing a really scary '70s outfit while giving the speech and pretending nothing is the matter...

Liz Allison
Voter
Garden City, New York

I remember a speech someone gave about how students were forced to use those tiny brown paper squares in the bathrooms while the faculty bathrooms had real toilet paper. I don't remember anything he said, but I remember him holding a roll of toilet paper he had stolen from the faculty bathroom in triumph! Sometimes a little symbolism that people will remember goes a lot further than a long meaningful speech.

Adrian Gell
Voter
LaGrangeville, New York

One boy used a story book theme. He walked up on stage with a tall red and white striped hat on his head. With a lot of confidence, he plopped himself down on the edge of the stage, feet dangling over, and pulled out a huge colorful book that he had made himself. The story went along the lines of "The Cat in the Hat." It talked about him, his qualifications, and even had a little storyline about the Cat in the Hat character trying to help him win this election. The book had the rhyming rhythm that Doctor Seuss used, and included large pictures that could be seen by all the audience, which he held up as if he were reading a bedtime story to children. It was extremely funny and very creative.

Krista Dillinger
Voter
Colorado Springs, Colorado

One year we were listening to speeches and there were a lot of candidates running. By the time my friend had gone up to give her speech, everyone was inattentive and talking loudly and had ignored the past three speeches that were given—every candidate's nightmare. So when she walked up to the podium to give her speech, she brought three or four balloons up to the microphone and popped all of them with a needle. Everyone was quiet and staring at her and she began her speech with, "Well, now that I have your attention..." She won the election and that is the one speech I still remember to this day.

Sheila Miller
Voter
Winter Park, Florida

During the speech, this candidate somehow left the stage with out anyone noticing him leave. Then, when it was time for him to come to the podium, you saw a black cardboard box "driving" out onto the stage area. His friends were in suits, standing like secret service men around the auditorium. The soon-to-be President walked out and gave a speech about the future of every individual (that some people will succeed and some will fail, and how some friends will separate over time and some will get closer, and even though bad things happen, we could always look back to the best year we had in high school). Then he talked about himself and the promises he would commit himself to, and how he would help make it a good year. The rest of the assembly was long and boring, but everyone remembered his name and what he did to get elected.

Betsy Hill
Voter
Richmond, Virginia

This only works with elementary school elections, in which most of the student body is very young and doesn't know the people who are running for offices. When I was 5 years old, there was a kid running for school President. I didn't even know him, but during his campaign speech, he did something very simple: he made a gigantic "sample" ballot and with one of those gigantic inflatable pencils he pretended to check off his name on the huge sample ballot he had written his name on. Every student who was under 10 years old thought that was a really cool thing, and he was the ONLY one we remembered, so we all voted for him. In an election in which you are dealing with really young kids, the only important thing is to make sure that they KNOW YOUR NAME. In most cases, it will be the only name on the ballot which they know.

Syd Gernstein
Voter
McLean, Virginia

In sixth grade, I gave a campaign speech where I brought in a grocery bag full of items that can be found at your typical grocery store. I started out by saying, "When I sat down to write my speech, my mom made me go to the grocery store, so all I have is this bag of groceries..." Then, I carefully took all the items out, one piece at a time, while saying a catchy phrase about each item. For example, "I will do the TOTAL job as President" [showing Total cereal]. I had about 10-15 products, like Pledge, Thank You cherry pie filling, and others like that. The speech helped me pull off a stunning upset against a more popular student for President of my grade school.

> *Michael Mills*
> *Student Body President*
> *Whitehouse, Ohio*

A kid who won the Class President election had a very interesting speech. His approach was sort of a "Here's what I'm willing to do for YOU!" kind of thing. What he did was take off his shoe and put all kinds of disgusting things in it, making jokes and anecdotes the whole time, then he put the shoe back on. Kids love that sort of stuff! They got all excited and laughed and said, "eeew gross." It was a blast! He won by a landslide. Of course, this was way back in elementary school...

> *Nicole Osborn*
> *Voter*
> *Chandler, Arizona*

One of the things a previous Student Body President did was he made a strange concoction of Coco, Wheaties, Syrup, Tabasco Sauce, and green peppers. He ate it and said nobody but a Student Body President who cared would do that.

> *Amanda A. Zahm*
> *Voter*
> *American Falls, Idaho*

Usually the Freshmen really don't know who to vote for because they're new to the school. So this girl used as her campaign manager a janitor that was very popular and that everyone knew, especially the Freshmen. She had him even come on air with her (during televised speeches) wearing her pins and buttons and signs and he was so funny that anyone who was undecided or didn't care voted for her, not because she was popular, but because she made it funny and got someone that everyone knew involved.

Jennifer Galipault
Student Council Treasurer
Fort Lauderdale, Florida

At one of the assemblies—a talent show or air-band or something—one of the popular basketball players did a Blues Brothers routine which was so awesome that everyone stood up and screamed for him and then talked about it for weeks. I didn't know this guy very well (he was 2 grades ahead of me), but I asked him one day if he would help me with my campaign by introducing me at the speeches assembly. I told him he could say "no" if he didn't want to, but he didn't mind at all. He was great. He loved the opportunity to get up in front of the students again, and I loved the "coolness factor" that rubbed off onto my campaign when he told the student body, in his own style, that they should all vote for me.

Frank Shepard
Student Council Vice-President
Turtle Bay, New York

A few years ago, one of the guys had guys in the background singing the whole time, "Vote for E-Train"—and he won overwhelmingly because it was a really good beat and an easy thing to remember. The dumb thing stuck in your head and people were singing it all day long.

Tammy Rosenberg
Student Body President
Raleigh, North Carolina

I remember one boy who added into his speech a funny joke about a teacher. It was all prearranged and the teacher had previously consented, so it was not offensive to anyone. That made everyone laugh and undoubtedly swayed some voters.

Jennifer Brown
Voter
Oxnard, California

A girl demonstrated everyone arriving in high school for the first day. She had the guys dress up as girls, and the girls dress up as guys, then she used them to act out little skits to illustrate, while she explained the things she would do to make high school year great and prosperous.

Charisse Dillon
Voter
Simi Valley, California

There was this guy running for Class President who was taking off his clothes while he was speaking, because as part of his speech, he kept saying, as he took off each piece, "I have nothing to hide! I have nothing to hide!" It was really funny. Everyone got a big laugh, and of course he won.

Julie Mufson
Voter
Ann Arbor, Michigan

At a pep rally we had, the guy swim team stripped to our speedos and ran around the gym, getting everyone going. Since we did that stunt without permission, they can now only take their shirts off... But I won the election by a landslide.

Dustin M. Houseman
Class President
York, Pennsylvania

I convinced 9 graduating Senior athletes to come out in front of the Senior class, rip off their shirts, and have D-O-U-G-4-P-R-E-Z spelled out on their chests. I handily won the election.

Doug Regner
Senior Class President
Tempe, Arizona

My friend Jessica, who won President of the entire school body, gave an election speech which was based on a theme of cooperation. In it, she had her boyfriend come up on stage and they did a swingdancing routine together (with a lot of cooperation needed for throwing the partner around and such). They were amazing, and people loved it! She then gave a short speech about cooperation, which was to be her main focus if she won the position... to work WITH the school administration and cooperate with not only them, but with the students as well.

Liberty Harper
Student Government Representative
Encinitas, California

The people who fared well were often not "the cool kids," but those who would demand attention during their campaigns. For example, the guy who won for Senior Class President worked off a Pulp Fiction / James Bond theme. He and his friends wore full suits to school the day of candidate speeches and voting. Then, during speeches, for his turn, there was just a chair out in the middle of the gym floor. Some 007 music began to play and a guy came out and placed a briefcase on the chair. Then he left and a few seconds later another guy came out, picked up the briefcase and sat down in the chair. He opened the briefcase and took out a letter. In the meantime, the music had softened up and a voice was reading the letter aloud. The letter stated why the class members should vote for this candidate (without trashing the other candidates) and the last line, in typical James Bond fashion, was "this letter will self-destruct in five seconds." The guy who was reading the letter jumped out of the seat and ran out of the gym... It was an effective campaign—it's been almost 2 years and I still remember it.

Anne Murphy
State House of Reps. Minority Leader
Boston, Massachusetts

IDEAS FOR POSTERS

Write your name on those little neon price tags and tie them to backpacks of your supporters.

Travis J. Wilson
President, National Honor Society
Glendale, California

I put door-hangers with my name on them on every door.

Crystal Pendleton
Freshman Class President
Fort Valley, Georgia

I hung signs from the ceiling, kinda like the signs hanging from overpasses... The first one said "vote," the second said "for," and the third said "Emily." Everyone told me they really liked them.

Emily Hartman
Voter
Broadlands, Illinois

We wrote with sidewalk chalk all over campus in huge letters a couple of times.

Emiley L. Erb
Voter
Chesapeake, Virginia

The morning of the election, I got to school at 6:00 AM armed with 206 strips of paper with my name on each piece. Every kid who would be voting that day had my name taped to their locker when they got to school that morning. My name was literally everywhere. (Double-sided tape is definitely recommended for this). I won the election by ten votes and am convinced that this last attempt won me the election.

Jessica Eule
Vice President of Senior Class
Parsippany, New Jersey

I bought a huge roll of white paper from an art supply store, and put big pieces of it down on my parents' front driveway (over spread-out newspapers), held down in the corners by rocks. Then I put a stencil I had made, which simply said "Lieberman for Vice" in big fancy letters, over them and spraypainted through the stencil. Instead of using only one color, though, I used different colors on each poster, with varied stripes and dots. They came out beautifully, each one was unique, and they were easy (and fun) to do. On the day of my speech, I wore a white t-shirt on which I had spraypainted the same thing through the stencil, so people who didn't know me could visually put together the posters and me.

Bill Lieberman
Student Council Vice President
Youngstown, Ohio

Our student body President during our Senior year wrote up this little "Toilet Talk" paper and put it in the stalls of the bathrooms! It had a list of things that were happening at our school that week, and at the bottom it asked us to vote for him!

Nicole Jaillet
Drama Club President
Reno, Nevada

Write a letter. Address it to the students. Introduce yourself, tell why you are running, what you'd like to accomplish, and any information that you'd be likely to include in your speech. Make the content colorful and bright. It allows people to get to know you before you give your speech, if they don't already know you. Print it in a nice computer font, on colored paper—then paste a copy of it on a bigger poster board.

Cecilia Cava
Voter
Salinas, California

Put your posters in great places. At the end of lunch lines are cool or maybe on the flag pole. Some place where people will notice.

Maynard James Keenan
Middle School President
Bedford, Massachusetts

My Sophomore year, there were three candidates named Grote, Berta, and Gray that ran "together" by having their names on the same posters and by supporting each other when they went up to give their speeches. They would take a sign from the school, such as "No street shoes on the gym floor" and place their own sign beside it, "Grote, Berta, and Gray don't wear street shoes on the gym floor." They put a sign up by all the Spanish classes that said, "Grote, Berta, y Gray son candidatos buenisimos." They had a sign in the Science building that said, "Grote, Berta, and Gray are a homogenous mixture."

Leanne Suber
Voter
Newnan, Georgia

A friend of mine and I, when we were both running for class office, together made blatantly cheesy campaign signs. My name is Pete, his name is Paul. So we wrote, "Peter, Paul, and.... YOU!!," and superimposed it on a picture we took before the homecoming dance last year when we were both dressed up. It was one of those "he's my bud and we're in suits" sort of pictures, which looked political yet hammy. Plain and simple: gratuitous humor and nonsense wins high school elections.

> *Pete Gerharz*
> *Senior Class Vice President*
> *Lombard, Ilinois*

There was this huge sign with a (real) boombox on it, playing music. So everyone wanted to know where this music was coming from, so their eyes were drawn to the sign. And sure enough, the creators of that advertisement are now the President and Vice-President of Student Senate. It worked for them!!

> *Kris Van Ness*
> *Voter*
> *Hudson, Wisconsin*

Someone put mirrors (actually, reflecting stickers) on posters with the caption, "Look who's voting for John Doe for Treasurer!"

> *Nicki Flax*
> *Voter*
> *Ft. Lauderdale, Florida*

My slogan was "pick a winner" and I drew pictures of people picking their noses or their "wedgies."

> *Maggie Graham*
> *Sophomore Class Officer*
> *Louisville, Kentucky*

Some ideas I've seen: the candidate's face on (1) a dollar bill (2) Uncle Sam (3) a muscleman (4) an actor/actress (5) the President of the United States.

Andy Beall
Voter
Worthington, Ohio

Two things to STAY AWAY FROM are the completely overused "K-I-M-B-E-R-L-Y: K is for Kindness, I is for Intelligence, M is for Maturity," etc. and "The recipe for a good class president: 1 cup of experience, 3 tablespoons of enthusiasm, a dash of energy," etc. These are so cutesy-annoying! Make your posters resemble your personality. Is that the kind of person you want to be seen as?

Kelli Hart
Voter
Houston, Texas

This one guy I ran against used his computer to put his head on President Clinton's body for flyers... Everybody loved it (of course, this was before the Clinton scandals...)

Michelle Quigley
Class President
Rockford, Illinois

I went to an all-male, Catholic, college preparatory school, and of course it was full of testosterone and raging hormones, so when I found myself falling behind in the polls, I made a stop at one of my favorite restaurants. Maybe you've heard of it, Hooters. Anyway, I took my camera to dinner with me that night, and half-way through the meal I told my waitress that it was my birthday, and I asked if I could get a picture taken with all of the waitresses to help remember this special occasion. Being the gracious person she was, she complied. I then took the picture to Kinko's, had several dozen enlarged copies made, and then posted them all around school advertising that if I were to be elected, then these beautiful babes would be the new lunch ladies. It was a long-shot, but it worked. My popularity shot through the roof in less than a week, and two weeks after that I was elected. Everyone knew I was lying, but they liked my attempt enough to vote for me.

Michael Popich
Student Council President
Columbus, Ohio

In one poster, I had a picture of a dorky guy who was stressing out. Next to this picture, I placed a picture of Quentin Tarantino with a girl on either arm. Over the dorky guy, I wrote "Before voting for Josh Stern." Over Tarantino I wrote "After voting for Josh Stern."

Joshua Stern
Senior Class President
Poughkeepsie, New York

One funny campaign poster read, "Vote for Mike and Marc, We're Just Two Regular Guys." Even though that was about three years ago, it stuck out in my mind over the years, because the picture of them was the two of them in a photo booth, picking their noses!!!

Theresa Pergola
Voter
Valley Stream, New York

A friend of mine put up posters saying something about the election. But, at the bottom of each one, he had a little thing saying, "paid for by the little old lady across the street" and other funny "paid for by" inside jokes. People talked about them and since no one cared about what the candidates stood for, people voted for him because he had funny posters...

Mike Tokarz
Class Vice President
Raynham. Massachusetts

One year this guy's campaign posters were "Ten Ways Student Council is like Sesame Street," one year it was "Ten Ways Student Council is like Baywatch" (both have great bodies, etc.), and once it was "Ten Ways Student Council is like My Awful Haircut." People looked forward to these unabashedly corny analogies, and I think the humor was what got him elected 3 years in a row.

Cynthia Kinnan
Voter
Golden, Colorado

One thing I saw that was really good was two people running together who got t-shirts made for about 15 bucks with both of their pictures and a slogan on back, which they wore the entire week before elections. It was a crack up.

John "Lo" Davis
Voter
Huntington Beach, California

One year I was running for Treasurer and I bought a bunch of play money, made copies of my picture to paste on the bills, and then pinned them on old hats. I brought the hats to school every day during election week and asked my friends and some of my teachers to wear them.

Daniel Colton
Student Body President
Scottsdale, Arizona

PART 3

MORE ADVICE
FROM
YOUR PEERS

SHOULD YOU RUN?

> ## You don't need to be popular to win a school election.

What won student elections in my school was a good sense of humor and respectability, not really popularity in a social sense.

Keith Zarriello
President
Suffern, New York

Those ultra-popular people won't win against the everyday person, because there are many more everyday people in school than ultra-popular people. If you get the vote of the everyday Joe and Bob, you've gotten the vote of the majority of the students. Everyday people don't want to see those ultra-popular people have positions of power. Everyday people should realize this and not hesitate to run for office!

Olivia Wood
Student Assembly Representative
Eastpointe, Michigan

Only about $^1/_5$ of the people are "cool." The other $^4/_5$ aren't. When election time comes, most students identify with the "uncool" candidate. "Cool" people are so picky about who they can or can't be friends with. "Uncool" people don't worry about impressing people, so they're friends with everyone. In the long run, the "uncool" people are more popular (have more friends) than the "cool" people. Isn't that weird?

> *Britnye Godwin*
> *Senior Class President*
> *Denver, Colorado*

I won a vice-president race against a popular person, as did two of my friends, for president and treasurer. I think people were sick of it being a popularity contest. We told the other students that we had ideas and that we would work hard for them. We told them to vote for who you think will do a good job, not just who you think is popular.

> *Nicholas LaVallee*
> *Junior Class Vice President*
> *Cornwall, New York*

Just remember, the popular people aren't always the ones we want to have power and the ability to make important decisions...

> *Jason Johns*
> *Voter*
> *Stockton, California*

The so-called "popular" people won all through junior high, but once I got to high school, the people that won were actually the people that had something good to say and got off their butts and actually did something.

> *Leah Barcaro*
> *Voter*
> *Altoona, Pennsylvania*

When I was a Junior, a student who wasn't very popular or well known ran, but she had a lot of confidence in herself. In her speech, she said that she knew she wasn't the most popular candidate, but she asked that we look beyond popularity and who's my friend, and look at who would be the best leader for our school. She won with probably 90 percent of the votes. She was able to make everyone realize that she could do the job, and all she needed was a chance. If a student can just be herself, instead of trying to put on a show, then the other students will see her sincerity, and will respect it. Most everyone will respect someone who is honest much more than someone who is cocky.

Craig Edwards
Voter
Greensboro, North Carolina

Most teenagers recognize that popularity is not going to get them anywhere if they don't have good ideas. Therefore, they vote for the candidate who has ideas, whether he/she is popular or not. People generally look to vote for the candidate who they think can deliver and help them the most.

Kathleen Tierney
Junior Class President
Natick, Massachusetts

Yes, elections are definitely a popularity contest—but not who one hangs out with or how many touchdowns one's scored, but rather how one presents oneself as a leader and a speaker. What makes a good teacher? Not how much they know, or where they went to school, but how they present the information. With elections it's the same thing. Any student who can present him or herself as comfortable in front of a large audience, can speak fluidly and casually, can keep a crowd alive with a little humor and down to earth points, and at the same time sell his or her campaign, can consider him or herself the next school president.

Robert O'Brien
Senior Council Senator
Portland, Maine

> Students get tired of seeing
> the same people always win.

It was always the same people who ran every year. Finally, some guy that no one knew ran for VP of Student Senate, and the tactic he used to win us over was his down to earth attitude. He didn't put on the "I'm-popular-therefore-I-must-win-it-all" front, like the others did. He also pointed out that it would be nice to see a different face in the office besides those we had seen for four years.

Michelle Adkins
Voter
Lee's Summit, Montana

People often get tired of seeing the same people win, especially when their heads grow to the size of a watermelon.

Misty L. Milby
Voter
Shelbyville, Kentucky

I ran against a three-time incumbent girl who was rather popular. This helped me, because people were sick of her. Many people wanted to see some fresh blood in the presidency, but nobody wanted to run against her, especially her popular friends.

Joshua Stern
Senior Class President
Poughkeepsie, New York

There is a guy who stutters and has a huge nose, who beat one of the prettiest girls in our class in an election, and here's why. People didn't want to see the girl win. Although she looked good, no one liked her as a person and she made a fool out of herself in her speech by acting like she would definitely win. He beat her, not because he was necessarily the best candidate, but because voters didn't want to see the other candidate get it.

Alison Comstock
Voter
Houston, Texas

In eighth grade, the winning election speech was by someone who didn't have a lot of friends and who no one would have normally voted for. He said something to the effect of, "elections need to be more than a popularity contest, so I want you to vote for the people who are nerds and want to work hard for our class, not the people who are in it just for the glory." It worked, they did, and he won.

Misty Rose Hitt
Class Vice-President
San Jose, California

The only reason I ever voted for anyone was because I knew them as a nice person. Pricks who are cocky are a total turn-off, even if they are my friends.

John Davis
Voter
Huntington Beach, California

> You absolutely can't win
> if you don't try.

My best advice would be that everyone should try. I didn't have any friends in my school but I decided to run for Government Group (it is a group of students in evenly-ranked offices that run the school). I ended up winning and being on this group, and it is really great. You can't predict what's going to happen unless you give up by deciding not to run. Try, it can't hurt.

Johanna Otto
Government Group
Big Bear City, California

Never give up. A friend of mine had run for Class President the year before and lost, by quite a bit. However, he ran again the next year, against the same person, and won by a landslide. Not because his competitor had done something to ruin her popularity, but simply because his classmates could see that he (my friend) was serious about the job itself. People have a lot of respect for someone who is out there to do something good without anything in return.

Jessica Dunaway
Voter
Springfield, Missouri

I ran for Class President in my high school against the most popular person I knew, and won. Believe in yourself, be genuine, don't try too hard, make friends with the people who aren't the most popular and work from there, but most importantly, have the desire to do it and the ability to be yourself. Don't sell yourself short.

Holly A. Smith
Junior Class President
Missoula, Montana

There is this one guy (probably the most popular guy in school) who thinks he's all that and was running for VP. He was being all cocky and saying stuff like, "Oh, no one wants to run against me?" Well, I'm not a popular person in school, but I do get along well with a lot of people. So I ran against him. When it was my opponent's turn to speak, he said some things that helped my chances for winning. He said stuff like, "I just think I have more experience than my opponent because I have been a class officer the past four years." When he said that, everyone was like "Ooooo!" and booing him. I simply smiled and motioned with my hand that he was going down. It made people laugh. When it was my turn to talk, I stated my name and the office I was running for and said, "I pretty much want the same things that all these other candidates want, but a big reason I'm running is that I just think it's about time somebody beat (the guy's name)." (Which was very true because he thinks that he can win at everything, because he has in the past.) They all cheered. I ended up beating him by a landslide, and I also found out that people I would have never thought would vote for me, did vote for me. When the results came in one of my friends told me that he just said, "I lost" in a confused expression, like he couldn't believe that I, an unpopular girl, beat the most popular guy in school. All I can say from my experience is to come across as a strong leader with confidence and to hold your ground. Don't feel discouraged. Know you're a winner, and you'll be the winner.

Melanie Bush
Vice President, National Honor Society
Borger, Texas

Have fun with the campaign and enjoy yourself. Then, even if you don't win, at least you can say that you had a great, fun-filled experience, and got to meet a lot of new friends!!!!

Lissette Lebrilla
Voter
Laguna Hills, California

Be yourself. No one can tell you what you can and can't do, so do what you believe in.

Abby Ruebusch
Voter
Bellevue, Washington

THE RIGHT ATTITUDE

BE YOURSELF! Be honest, be sincere, be genuine.

Our Class President is very popular because he knows how to run our class, and everybody likes him. He is very emotional and caring. It's how you are and how you act that makes you win.

John C. Van Norman
President, Key Club
Troy, Michigan

MOST IMPORTANT!!!!!! Do not, under any circumstances, try to make yourself appear to be somebody you're not... Not only do people see right through it, but it makes you look like a fool when they do.

Shannon Hinkle
Class President
Clarksville, Indiana

It's best for a student to be him or herself when running for an office. If a person takes on a different personality while running, it shows that this person isn't very sincere.

Matt Litz
President
Bellwood, Pennsylvania

My co-President and I got to our positions by just acting naturally during the election. We acted like ourselves and didn't make any false promises. We made only realistic promises that we could keep, i.e., if any of the group members needed any information that they missed or wanted, I said that they could come to me at any time and any place and I would give it to them. I kept that promise and was always real, not fake.

Vanessa Harrison
Co-President, Minneapolis Urban League
African American Student Organization
Minneapolis, Minnesota

Well, my friend thought for sure she was going to win the position of President and she didn't. The reason she didn't is because she was one of those types who always had to be right or knew everything. And everybody liked her—or so she thought—but they didn't all vote for her. She tried too hard to be everybody's friend. Sometimes she doesn't act like herself, she puts on a show. That is the reason the other person won. You have to totally be yourself, and people will like you and accept you for who you are.

Christy Wadley
Voter
Athens, Michigan

First of all, the people to be elected MUST come across real. They have to be genuine. None of those ugly, fake smiles like people do when they wanna be elected. They have to be somewhat cool, dress casual but nice at the same time, and during a speech, give the audience a feeling of relation to the speaker—like they're one of them.

Michael Crosswhite
Voter
Belleview, Florida

Be yourself. People can see right through you when you're acting.

Kenneth G. Pittman
State Mu Alpha Theta Treasurer
Knoxville, Tennessee

You need to be truthful... otherwise people think you're fake and that really doesn't help you win. Be yourself, otherwise, people think your speech is fake, and then they start to think that the things you promise or hope to change won't happen... and you'll lose.

Julie Cameron
Voter
Canton, Michigan

I won the Secretary race at a school I had only been at for one year. The main thing needed to win a school election, I think, is an honest and sincere campaign. You need to know what the students want and you cannot be judgmental of people who are not like you. Through all of it, I have gained a lot of friends who are all so different.

Katie Straw
Student Body Secretary
Fort Smith, Arkansas

Don't promise things you can't deliver and don't say things just because you think it's what others want to hear. You'll be appreciated so much more if you're an honest person.

Shaneen Rowe
SGA Executive Board Member
Rochester, New York

Be honest and truthful about what you can actually do once you're in office, don't just say what you think they want to hear and then not fulfill your promises. Nobody likes a liar, and everyone can tell when you're just going through the motions and don't really believe in what you're saying.

Amanda Doss
FBLA Treasurer
Bossier City, Louisiana

The most important thing that people can do is have a passion for their subject. I would have to say the winners at my school were almost always the people who had a genuine passion for what they were running for.

Lindsey Sherline
Voter
Beverly Hills, Michigan

I believe that the most important thing is to be honest. If you are running for an office and someone asks you your opinion about a topic, give it to them honestly, even if your viewpoint doesn't happen to agree with theirs or with the majority of your school's. People will respect you for not lying to them to get their vote.

Sean Carano
Class President
Maple Heights, Ohio

I find that the most important aspect of any candidate is how sympathetic and compassionate he/she is rather than how intelligent, powerful, or persuasive. The best candidate is somebody the students can relate to—which usually is NOT the most elite and popular one.

Gina Protopapa
President, National Honor Society
Cuyahoga Heights, Ohio

Be a friendly "people person" and talk to everyone.

If the person you're running against thrives in a very selective clique, then chances are, the people in that clique are the only ones that like him/her, and even that's not a given. A candidate who's a real "people person," someone who hasn't pissed a lot of people off, is more likely to win than a social ladder climber.

Josh Barnett
Voter
Silverton, Oregon

You need to be a people person, in the sense that you need to be upbeat and friendly with everybody, not just the popular people. Even the little guy has a vote which counts just as much as the prom queen's.

Joey Lesch
Club Vice President
Denver, Colorado

Three things you must be when running for office are honest, outgoing, and friendly to everyone.

Andrea Miller
Voter
Lexington, Massachusetts

One word—NETWORK. If you know a lot of people, you have a better chance of getting help in your campaign and a much better chance of achieving your goals. Don't overlook the importance of one-on-one contacts.

Steve Ward
State Master Councilor,
Palmetto DeMolay Association
Walterboro, South Carolina

Make friends. Befriend anyone and everyone that you can. Meet people from all of the cliques and make sure they know that you are a good person. In school, no one really cares about qualifications or promises, but more who is your friend.

Kenneth J. Conley
Class President
Winter Park, Florida

The candidates who are very uptight give people the feeling that they are kind of sneaky and deceptive. The person I was going against was popular and had a lot of friends, but was very snobbish to the people not in her "group." The more friendly approach helped me win.

Jayme Elizabeth
Class President
Philadelphia, New York

The so-called dorks in school always seem to outnumber the popular kids, and their votes count just as much. Be nice to EVERYONE. Don't wait for the election to do this, though, or people will think it's funny. Be friendly all year round.

> *Jessica Eule*
> *Senior Class Vice President*
> *Parsippany, New Jersey*

One thing that stands out in people that I look to elect for Student Council is the fact that they're simply friendly with everyone, no matter what the other people are like. Ya know? Someone who doesn't judge people on anything but their personalities and is open to be social with everyone.

> *Charlie Meister*
> *Voter*
> *Lancaster, New York*

I have noticed that the nicest, friendliest people do win. The best thing to do in school is be nice to EVERYONE, even that jerk that is so rude to you in class and thinks he rules the school.

> *Michelle Leigh*
> *Voter*
> *Pearland, Texas*

I found the one thing that really puts you ahead in an election is just being nice. I found that what my classmates really wanted was a leader who was not only responsible, but also approachable and kind. As they say, "It's nice to be important, but it's more important to be nice."

> *Meg Wynstra*
> *Junior Class President*
> *Walnut Creek, California*

I had a friend who won every year of her high school career because she was nice to everyone. She would say hi to every single person she saw, and talk to you even if you weren't "cool." She basically became good friends with everyone by being herself and being kind to all.

Brian P. Hamlett
Voter
Kannapolis, North Carolina

I was the type of person who was friends with everyone, or at least knew everyone and talked to everyone. It helped that I was nice to the "less popular" people, because they have just as much influence in voting as the "more popular" ones.

Elizabeth Sigmond
Class President
Wales, Wisconsin

When it comes down to it, the kids who have the most determination and skill along with a nice and casual personality usually come out on top. The know-it-all so-called "shoo-ins" have very rarely won over these deserving people.

Liberty Harper
Student Government Representative
Encinitas, California

Start as EARLY as possible!

Go and take the time ahead of elections to get to know people, not just at the last minute. It won't hurt to eat with someone different at lunch or to help out someone you don't know. When the time comes that the other candidates rush to get votes, they will usually remember how you paid attention to them even before the elections, not just as an empty attempt to win their vote. The key is to talk to everyone.

Russ Bullock
Student Council Representative
Antioch, California

Don't be fake. Don't go up and talk to all sorts of people in a cheery sort of way just because it is election time. Sincerity is a key to success.

Lisa Norlander
Class Vice President
Cupertino, California

There is nothing worse than a phony candidate. A person should never try to become friends with the entire school the week before elections. You should be genuine and friendly 100% of the time rather than just during election time, or people will see right through you.

Lori DelliColli
Vice-President of Freshman and
Sophomore Class
Methuen, Massachusetts

People notice when one day you don't even talk to them, then when elections come around, suddenly they're your best friend. People are not as dumb as they look!! Be nice but "be yourself."

Brooke Coniam
Voter
Tarpon Springs, Florida

> ## Strive to be a peer, not a politician.

Try to be yourself. Acting all super-nice all of a sudden is going to lose you votes, not gain them. Nobody wants to elect a fake. Also, try to relate to all the people in the school, not just the "cool" ones.

Kelly McCann
Class Historian
Jacksonville, Florida

If you act like a common student, not like you are some God or something, students will relate to you better. Don't talk like you are a teacher, but also don't talk like you are some homey off the street. A touch of businessman in your speech will show the students that you are responsible, but do NOT act above them. Try to be sincere and talk personally to students, and most importantly, listen to them!

Greg Plotner
Student Body Vice President
Lancaster, Pennsylvania

Avoid "polish" and "gloss," and instead offer the voting public something they've probably never seen before: student-minded students running for office, as opposed to the standard political mold.

Michael Pristash
SGA President
Northfield, Minnesota

Ass kissing is a definite "turn-off" to a voter...

Bryna Warnock
President of Beta Club
Pensacola, Florida

An obnoxious guy came up to me and introduced himself. He was so fake, I quote, as he shook my hand, "Hi, I'm (name) and I'm running for governor. If I could get your support I could help you out if you need a job." I watched him give the same line over and over again like a robot. Let's just say he lost. Don't give a rehearsed "pitch." Be yourself and be open to the world around you.

Christopher F. Heck
Voter
Fairborn, Ohio

Be real... smile, laugh, treat voters as equals... just don't try to blatantly flatter them with compliments or anything like that, because that just makes you look phony.

Christina Littlefield
Voter
Hampton, Virginia

Don't get glamorous. The superstar act doesn't do the trick. It's the down-to-earth people who aren't trying to get into Hollywood with their campaigns who really catch my eye.

Kristi Cradduck
Voter
DeKalb, Illinois

The person who won a huge election at my college was the one who was GENUINELY nice and sincere when he talked to you. He didn't try to "sell" himself, he just had a conversation. When elections came around, everyone knew him as a friendly guy and during his speech, he didn't have to try to show people the real him... He had already done it.

Beth A. Zermani
Co-President of French Club
Saugus, Massachusetts

My best friends are some of the leaders of the school. The way they won was by simply being friendly. They don't fit in to just one group of people, they're very universal and will talk to anybody. They aren't the best people in the world, they're just normal. They don't try to be anybody they're not, and it works. Their speeches were very conversational. They didn't seem to try to be too cool for everybody, which has been the major pitfall of people that have lost elections in our school. Instead, they won by just connecting with students.

Patrick Hagan
Voter
Signal Mountain, Tennessee

The most important thing is to be calm about the whole thing. Don't get uptight and take it too seriously. Remember it's just school.

Daniel Colton
Student Body President
Scottsdale, Arizona

Have fun! Not everyone does this.

> Rebecca Gillette
> Student Council Treasurer
> Marathon, New York

> ## Don't try to make your opponents look bad. It just makes you look like a jerk.

The one thing that turned me off right away to a campaign was dirty politics. The worst thing you can do is try to make the other person look bad to make yourself look good. People don't want to hear about the other person's downfalls, they only want to hear about what you can do to make your school/group better.

> Sylvia Yolinsky
> Voter
> Washington, DC

Do NOT bash your opponent—that gives the opponent a sympathy effect and makes you look bad.

> Brett R. Laurence
> Senior Class Treasurer
> Kennett Square, Pennsylvania

Don't slander the other candidate. You lose respect, and ultimately the undecided voters will see you as a jerk who'll be unable to take advice or keep an open mind when they have suggestions.

> Jeff McMahon
> Freshman Executive Committee
> Baton Rouge, Louisiana

NEVER put down your opponent in front of other people. You're not fighting with someone. You're simply trying to earn a title with your intelligence, not your sarcasm.

Melissa Lewis
Voter
Philo, Ohio

At one of my school elections, this one girl made a rude remark about the person running against her, and I think that's what kept her from being President of my Senior Class. Everyone in my class at first thought that she was really nice, but after she said the rude remark, everyone thought differently and she didn't win.

Laura Staples
Voter
Rochester, New York

There was one kid who was mocking another student behind her back while the other student was giving her speech... He was really popular, but this made him look like an idiot and someone who didn't care about anyone but himself.

Catrina L. Morris
Voter
Kennewick, Washington

The worst thing I have seen in a high school election is the name calling and teasing of the other candidates. It shows that you aren't really worried about what you can do for us, only how you can make this candidate look bad for your own good.

Ashleigh Dempton
DCT District Secretary
Mount Dora, Florida

Don't say bad stuff about the other candidates, it just makes you sound like a bad person to have in office.

Jay Covey
Voter
Wooster, Ohio

Be nice—do not badger your opponent. Even if he does it to you, don't sink to his level.

Shaneen Rowe
SGA Executive Board Member
Rochester, New York

A candidate was purposefully sabotaging my friend's campaign. She and her friends tore down posters and tried to make my friend look bad. In the end, this only hurt her, because people heard what she did and there was a bad reaction to her behavior. Treat the other candidates as you wish to be treated. Play fair, and make it known that that is the way you want it to be.

Mary Smith
Voter
Chesterfield, Virginia

Someone running for office should be calm and relaxed and should have no clue about the other candidates or how they are doing. Concentrate on your own campaign only. Remember that it is a Student Council campaign, not a war! Don't be mean to the other person, because people see will the harsh criticism and think you're hitting below the belt.

Christopher J. Collins
Student Council President
Corpus Christi, Texas

> Be confident and positive,
> but don't get cocky or arrogant.

Be confident!!! If you have a positive attitude about yourself and believe in yourself, you have a better chance of succeeding.

Katie Armacost
Voter
Reisterstown, Maryland

Confidence is the key to selling yourself.

Christina Jones
Voter
Coppell, Texas

If you feel confident about yourself and the goals that you have set, others will too. People can read you better than you think, and if you get up there with a confident attitude and good composure, others will feed off of that. If you seriously believe that you are the best person for the job, then others will too. The first step to success is believing in yourself.

Laura Gottlieb
B'nai B'rith Chapter President
Solon, Ohio

It is extremely important to be confident. If the candidate looks like he/she can handle anything, you know that he/she won't freak out if an unexpected problem occurs.

Erica Charlene
Voter
Turlock, California

Confidence and the ability to assure voters that their needs will be met is a good thing, but simply saying that you've got the highest grades of anyone and are on every cool team or something like that is a major turn off. If the candidate at the podium seems to think that she's better than everyone else, it will immediately turn many voters off.

Kris Long
Class Vice-President
Davie, Florida

Do NOT be overconfident. People will not vote for pompous windbags.

Steve Ward
State Master Councilor,
Palmetto DeMolay Association
Walterboro, South Carolina

Most people who win the elections at my school act as though they've won weeks before the actual vote. This, of course, can be taken too far and can backfire. No one wants a smug or arrogant leader.

Jane Holsapple
Voter
Lincoln, Nebraska

I would not vote for anyone who looks and sounds like a jerk. I know it is easy to say, but if you go into anything with the attitude that you are better than everyone else, you come off as ignorant and conceited. You have to appeal to the people and, most importantly, be excited about what you are doing. Don't get me wrong, you need to go into it with a winning attitude, just not an "I'm-better-than-everyone-else" attitude.

AJ Renchin
Secretary, National Honor Society
Lakeville, Minnesota

Never act like you know you're going to win, even if you know the other person is a complete geek. People don't like cockiness.

Christy Harrington
Voter
Newcastle, Oklahoma

One cocky kid actually got up there and said, "Vote for me, I am the best and I will be the best for the school Vice-President!" He lost though.

Brooke Marlee
Senior Class Treasurer
Cleveland, Ohio

Although the "cool" guy had the votes of his "cool" friends, the people who didn't know him didn't vote for him. Never get overconfident and think you have won till the votes are in...

Fernando Hernandez
Voter
Manhattan Beach, California

Always remember, you CAN be beat. Once you think you are a sure bet, the other person will win.

Benjamin King
Senior Class President
Pittsburg, Texas

Never assume you are going to win. When you are too sure of yourself, you end up not doing enough to promote yourself.

John E. Parman
presidential candidate
Berkeley, California

Don't be stuck up. Last year, a friend of mine won Student Council President against someone who had been President for 2 years. The one who lost had the attitude that he would win no matter what, which turned people off. The one who won was very friendly to people and talked to everybody, even those he didn't know, even if he only said, "Hey, please vote for me." He did a lot of campaigning and obviously wanted it more, and people knew that.

Tom Healy
Voter
Silver City, New Mexico

The worst thing you can do is just assume you'll win the election. A boy ran for the Senior Class Treasurer against one of my good friends. He was popular and VERY arrogant. My friend was not popular at all, so everyone assumed she'd lose. She tried hard and campaigned while the boy just sat back and assumed he'd win. Even in his speech, he didn't act like he cared. My friend, on the other hand, was very sincere and really cared. She won the election by a landslide.

Elisa Wall
Senior Class Secretary
Trafalgar, Indiana

A GREAT SPEECH

Don't be overly serious.

Most people automatically think a speech is going to be boring. So you have to have some sort of gimmick to get their attention. Humor relaxes people so they're more open to what you have to say.

Bob Weber
Jogs Officer
Mantua, Ohio

A speech needs to contain more funny stuff in it than serious stuff. It should give the idea that the students are in control and not the teachers.

Crystal Crowell
Voter
Whitehall, Ohio

You have to entertain the voters rather than impress them with speeches on how responsible you are. A kid will vote for you because you were that funny guy that made him crack up. You can't take yourself too seriously.

Andrew Ells
President of Freshman Class
Mesa, Arizona

The main thing is the candidate. You have to make yourself likeable and relate to people. Speeches that totally bore people are no good.

Crystal Capps
Voter
Sharon, Tennessee

Speech after speech all said the same old stuff until this kid came along who no one had really ever heard of before. His speech was different. He used music and really caught everyone's attention. He managed to get everyone interested and listening. He won Class Secretary that year and was re-elected again the next year. Be different, and get your point across QUICKLY.

Mellisa Lucido
Voter
Sterling Heights, Michigan

Get the student body involved in your speech and make it something people will talk about on their way out of the auditorium.

Keri Henderson
Music Society Secretary
Richmond, Virginia

Those who aren't afraid of looking stupid in front of an audience consisting 100% of their peers... those who can be loud and stupid—or if they keep their speech REAL short... they'll win.

Dipali Patel
Voter
Davis, California

Never be afraid to make an ass out of yourself. Remember it is just high school, and have fun with it. After all, fun should be an important part of high school.

Ed Averett
Voter
Mercer Island, Washington

> You're not being graded.
> Remember why you're there
> and who you're talking to.

Use commonly-used words. Don't use complicated words only a Yale student knows. Most of the public, unless they are English teachers, don't have that big of a vocabulary.

Calvin Cheong-Yuen Ng
Voter
Alameda, California

Be casual, not stuffy like some professor. After all, it is only high school, and students want to have fun.

Anne Portugal
Voter
Daly City, California

Never treat an audience like they are children. Don't talk down to them.

Danielle Lynch
President, National Honor Society
Hoboken, New Jersey

One mistake I have seen almost every year is people trying to be too professional—using big words, trying to sound like they're running for President of the United States... A speech needs to be toned-down a little to make people listen. Kids my age don't pay attention to speeches on Capitol Hill, so why should a school election speech sound like one?

Chris Manley
Voter
Colorado Springs, Colorado

High school students don't want to be formally talked to by their peers. It makes them feel inferior. A nice informal speech that can be remembered with ease will help a lot.

Timothy A. McKnight
Voter
Palos Heights, Ilinois

Formality in speeches is boring to students. If the audience knows they are electing someone who has a good sense of humor and isn't all about business, they'll believe in their leader's capabilities a little more.

Nickole Rucker
Class President
Denver, Colorado

No one really took any of the elections seriously. We ended up voting for our friends or for the person that had the most unique speech. People who say things like "I would try to make our school a better place" usually don't really mean it, and say it only because it is the "traditional" speech. You shouldn't just say things you think people expect to hear. Be spontaneous.

Sheryl Reniva
Voter
Union, New Jersey

But don't try too hard. I remember a big mistake some girl in our high school made. She wasn't down with the "lingo," so in her speech, I guess she tried to be "cool" and she started off with "What's Up?" and ended her speech with "Seee Yaaa!" Someone else might have been okay doing that, but it made her look like a wannabe. Just be yourself. Don't be boring, but don't go overboard to the point where you look ridiculous.

Sara Caamano
Voter
Paterson, New Jersey

I found that if you address them as your friends and peers (which they ARE), they will relate and trust you.

Michael Halpin
Senior Class Vice President
Voorheesville, New York

> Don't expect your speech to miraculously come together while you're up there. Prepare and practice it beforehand!

The big thing when getting up in front of a crowd is to be completely prepared and confident. You need to know what you are saying and believe honestly in everything you are speaking about. I've heard a lot of fine speeches which died in their carry-out. It's important to practice and know what you're going to say so you can concentrate on communicating with the audience.

Tiffany Novinger
Senior Class Secretary
Harrisburg, Pennsylvania

The speeches count the most. My opponent had a solid speech (just before voting was to take place). My speech was good too, but there was one problem: I had left it in my car. True story. At the mike, I stumbled around and lost the election in the process. The next year, I stapled my speech to my shirt, and walked around all day with it there.

> *Kyle Rossi*
> *Class Treasurer*
> *Solon, Ohio*

In the speech, don't try to stretch out jokes. Practice your speech in front of a few friends first, and if they like your jokes, use them—if not, they most likely won't be funny to anyone else either.

> *Daniel Colton*
> *Student Body President*
> *Scottsdale, Arizona*

Practice your campaign speech in front of someone affiliated with theatre performance—they can usually help you get rid of the presentational "stuff" and help you be more believable and more effective.

> *Jonathan Conver*
> *Voter*
> *Louisville, Kentucky*

I remember a guy who ran for president who, for whatever reason, proclaimed that he didn't need his speech and tossed the pieces of paper that contained his speech on the ground. He started out decently, but soon started mumbling and sputtering out incoherent phrases. He almost literally dived for his written-speech, and then proceeded to read it for about five minutes in a monotone, unenthusiastic voice. He lost, badly. Moral of the story: don't do anything you're not fully prepared to do, or you'll look extremely bad in front of the voters.

Joe Kaufman
Voter
Scarsdale, New York

> To be comfortable and natural while speaking in front of an audience, just speak from the heart about what you're saying, and don't worry about speaking "correctly."

The first time I ran for an office, I was terrified. To get up in front of 400 of your peers and give a speech is completely nerve-wracking. The best thing to do is just to start talking. The opening line is the hardest part. Once you've gotten through that, you will be okay. The further you get into your speech the easier it gets. All you have to do is tell yourself to calm down and just start talking.

Sarah Payne
Student Council Vice-President
Mountlake Terrace, Washington

Just be yourself, don't read from a script where everything sounds like your English teacher wrote it. Just be straightforward and speak with a sure sound in your voice.

Randy Hart
Voter
Dallas, Texas

Don't start out your speech like, "Hello my name is Kate and I am here to talk to you about...."

Joshua Clements
Voter
Mount Holly, North Carolina

The "next year will be really cool if I win" speeches never work, at least they don't make the difference. What really worked at my school this year was a guy giving a speech that was genuinely from his heart.

Emily Haverkamp
Voter
Overland Park, Kansas

The best speech that I ever saw was delivered on the fly. Our current Student Council President stood up in front of the student body and was very natural. He introduced himself and said that he wanted to have fun his senior year and that he had been passive about his high school for too long. He wanted to get something done. The way to make people hear you in a speech is to just be yourself and speak from the heart about an issue you care about. I'm sure that you've heard that before, but it's true.

Joan Kisthardt
Senior Class Representative
Princeton, New Jersey

In the best speech I ever saw, the speaker went up and instead of standing behind the podium, she removed the microphone and walked around the gym in front of the audience. She seemed so relaxed, so comfortable. She had everyone's attention.

Lyle Krannichfeld
Voter
Sacramento, California

One of the candidates for president went on stage and gave practically an extemporaneous speech. She had no note cards. She spoke right from the heart. Everyone was in awe. She was elected to the position. That type of speech isn't for everyone, but she played it off very well.

Kelly A. Adams
Voter
Bucks County, Pennsylvania

A friend of mine won a school election a few years ago although he was the underdog. He was not popular, just a down-to-earth, really nice guy. Unlike the other candidates, who paraded around with big (fake) smiles on their faces, Bill just showed people his true nature. People were more receptive to him because he was simple and honest. Come election day, he stood at the podium and began his speech with a few pieces of paper in front of him. Then he walked away from the podium with the microphone and delivered an address that was straight from the heart. By the time he was finished, most everyone in the audience had given their vote to Bill. Simple, nice, honest... that was his winning combination.

Eric Green
Voter
Harrisburg, Pennsylvania

Some ways to be more comfortable while giving a speech

WHAT SHOULD YOU WEAR for your speech? Something that makes you comfortable, which you THINK makes you look good. It doesn't matter how you look as much as it matters how you feel. So wear something that will make you FEEL that you look good. If you feel confident about yourself, it will show.

Brett Skee
Class President
Gainesville, Florida

You should always speak slowly and let your words come out understandably without rushing. Gesture and make eye contact with the audience too, and don't just read from a sheet. Keep your composure and don't laugh when everyone else is laughing— deadpan is MUCH funnier!

Jeremy Gorelick
Club President
Greenlawn, New York

Always keep your eyes on your audience! It's best to come with a paper you never have to read. Just learn the important parts of your speech and talk naturally. If you ever feel you are forgetting something, take a quick look at your paper while talking. Don't stay silent for too long or it makes people think you are unsure and nervous. Also, a smile never costs anything and it's one of the most effective things you could do in a speech.

Dematte Arnaud
Voter
France

If you have note cards or a script to look at while talking, and you know about bad habits you tend to fall into while speaking (talking too fast, tapping your fingers, or other things to that effect), write these things on your cards, such as, "slow down" or "fingers?" in big bold letters, as reminders.

Miciala Marie Haight
Public Speaking and
Extemporaneous Speaking Captain
Flagstaff, Arizona

Write funny little notes in the margins of your speech (inside jokes or funny faces). They'll help you be less nervous and they might also help you smile.

Tiffany Mullan
School "Green Team" captain
Brooklandville, Maryland

If you have your entire speech written out in front of you, when you're nervous, you might tend to stick to it like glue. Then again, never go up to a speech empty-handed. Always have something to keep you on track, but not the whole thing word-for-word. The best thing is to have notes with just a few phrases to jog your memory, and then talk naturally about each thing. Once you get started, it's easy, if you've practiced a bit. If you absolutely must have more notes, as a security blanket, then circle or highlight a few key words in each section so that you can glance down and get the idea and not be tempted to read from it. Use your finger to keep your place so you can look at the audience without being afraid of getting lost.

Traci Marx
Student Council President
Fort Lauderdale, Florida

You can ease the crowd by relaxing yourself. If you're relaxed, instead of nervous and tense, it's so much easier for everyone to watch and absorb what you're saying.

Matthea Wilson
Voter
New Haven, Indiana

When doing a speech, just talk to the audience, don't read to them.

Rick Quitoriano
Voter
El Monte, California

Speak slowly and clearly.

Brooke Coniam
Voter
Tarpon Springs, Florida

Don't forget to breathe.

Annabel Cortez
Voter
Oxon Hill, Maryland

Never stop in the middle of your speech or admit that you messed up and get frazzled. Always keep going. Also, never get mad at the audience or try to shush them. The audience is made up of your friends and the people who will vote for you, not "the enemy."

Maynard James Keenan
Middle School President
Bedford, Massachusetts

When I made a mistake, I didn't try to cover it up, but rather I made a little joke, saying "Oops, that's not what I practiced" or something like that...

John Murphy
Voter
Phoenixville, Pennsylvania

A new boy went up to the front of the auditorium and before he got to the podium, he bumped into a fire extinguisher on the wall and it fell. He turned bright red and then began his speech by saying, "I meant to trip into that fire extinguisher, cause I know that you will remember my speech: the guy who tripped and made a complete fool of himself!"

Jayme Krausman
Voter
Rye Brook, New York

> The confidence you demonstrate while you're speaking is just as important as what you're saying.

Always have your speech planned out, usually in outline format. Walk to your place being certain to look as relaxed as possible. Be confident. If you don't convince your voters that YOU believe you can do the job and that you're glad to be there, they won't vote for you.

Marty Black
Senior Class President
Metairie, Louisiana

People look for sincerity. If your heart's in a speech, then your feelings will flow out of you and into the audience.

S. Kyle Overstreet
Student Council President
White Oak, Texas

People can sense fear, so you have to be confident. Always try to give a speech that you're comfortable with, so you feel confident when giving it.

Bob Weber
Jogs Officer
Mantua, Ohio

When you are lecturing or addressing people, you have to be in charge. If you don't know what you are doing, or if you're afraid of it, it will be very obvious. You have to take charge of the situation.

Nathan Hart
Voter
Leicestershire, England

If you feel confident in yourself, almost any speech is effective. It's like "Wow, that guy actually knows what he's talking about, he's not just reading from a piece of paper." People look for the confidence in speeches. If you appear on stage with sheets and sheets of paper in your hand, and you're shuffling your feet around, all sweaty and stuff, what kind of image does that give?

Anne Portugal
Voter
Daly City, California

The one speech that stuck out in my head above all others was one where a guy got up and chose not to use the microphone. His voice carried well, and he had a good speech to go along with it. It made him look very confident and well prepared. Plus, it was something out of the norm during the speeches, so people paid attention more.

Kristin Baldwin
Voter
Beaverton, Oregon

Eye contact is incredibly important to reading someone's genuineness. Keeping your eyes visible to everyone makes you appear grounded, firm and determined.

> *Jonathan Conver*
> *Voter*
> *Louisville, Kentucky*

When you are up in front of the audience, stay calm and be confident. Have the attitude that you are a winner and no one will beat you—but don't get too caught up with yourself.

> *Amy Feiner*
> *Voter*
> *Grand Blanc, Michigan*

Don't be nervous when you're going to do a speech because we're all human and we all make mistakes so don't worry about it.

> *Kari Kloc*
> *Student Council Representative*
> *Chicago, Illinois*

Be calm, address the students as though you were talking to good friends. Talk about things that mean a lot to you. Your sincerity will come through.

> *Karen Putman*
> *Student Council President*
> *Canton, Ohio*

Be confident as you face the crowd. Don't let them see fear or nervousness in you. This will give you credibility and trust. I've seen people give speeches which are shy and kind of timid. If they can't talk to us about why they're the right person for the job, how can they talk for us?

> *Michael Lee*
> *Vice President of Student Association*
> *Portland, Tennessee*

Never start your speech with, "Hi, my name is Ralph and I'm running again for President. Ummm... I know nothing got accomplished last year, but..."

> *Rhianna Meadows*
> *Voter*
> *Gorham, Maine*

Before you get up in front of people, just relax and take a few deep breaths. Don't do anything strange like thinking about the audience in their underwear or anything like that. Just keep in mind that they're just students like you. Who cares if they don't like your speech? You talked about something you thought was important, and if they don't like it then it's not a big deal. Try to keep the stress down.

> *Eric Ross*
> *Voter*
> *Escondido, California*

> Don't list everything you've ever done—nobody cares. Keep it SHORT, or you'll lose your audience.

Keep your speech short, entertaining, and to the point.

> *Stephanie Schaefer*
> *Senior Class Treasurer*
> *Denver, Colorado*

High school students have a very short attention span, so long speeches are a SERIOUS no-no. Keep it to less than 5 minutes, preferably shorter than that. Just get your point across and sit down. Be enthusiastic, and if you get the option, go last.

> *Lyle Krannichfeld*
> *Voter*
> *Sacramento, California*

Make your speeches short, simple, and to the point because a lengthy speech will make people get bored and lose interest. The average person's attention span is about four minutes, and nobody likes a windbag.

> *Christy Frey*
> *Voter*
> *Tampa, Florida*

Keep your speech short and to the point. Also, start your speech off by saying it will be short and to the point, and you may get lots of positive response.

> *Denise Levels*
> *Voter*
> *Oakland, California*

Yes, say why you are qualified for that particular position, but people don't want to hear about every single school club or organization you've been in. Just keep it brief.

> *Jessica Wilson*
> *School Student Council*
> *Clarksburg, West Virginia*

Describe what you plan to do in the position you are running for. Some credentials are important, but keep it to a very minimum.

> *Rebecca Gillette*
> *Student Council Treasurer*
> *Marathon, New York*

Long, boring speeches full of information that people do not want to hear really turn students off. I have heard a few speeches that were enthusiastic, decently short, and made an impact. Talk to the audience so they understand you, as if you were talking to only one person. When people feel they have something in common with you, they tend to understand and support you more.

Honey Diaz
Voter
Boston, Massachusetts

> **Talk about real issues and what you plan to do for the school.**

The people I was running against campaigned like crazy with stickers and all that stuff. I think what it came down to was the speeches. I won by addressing an issue that was of concern (that I knew our class was tired of hearing the negatives about them, and that I would lead the class in having a lot more school spirit). The others gave long boring speeches about how qualified they were, and promised things that would obviously never happen. Your speech must be short and to a specific point that is of interest and concern to the students, otherwise no one will listen or care.

Aaron Rhyne
Senior Class President
Westminster, Colorado

People talked in their speeches about how qualified they were. But since everyone was pretty much equally qualified, it just became a popularity contest. If I or any else had taken a different approach, and just talked about the people they would be representing, they would have won. You need to relate to the audience, talk to them about participation in the organization and what you want to do FOR THEM. Not just about you.

Evan Saona
Voter
Amherst, New York

If you can show that you can improve the school, you will be elected. Many times in a speech, candidates dwell on themselves and why they "should" be President or Vice-President. People don't care why YOU want to, they want a reason why THEY should want you in office.

John E. Parman
Voter
Berkeley, California

A speech defines the candidate to the student body and is the most important element of the campaign. It's where elections are lost or won. Unfortunately, the general student body is not interested in school politics (or they'd be running themselves), so it's the candidate's job to interest them. Try to involve them by bringing up issues they'll care about.

Robert O'Brien
Senior Council Senator
Portland, Maine

Tell more of how you would help the school out. Not many people really did that. It was mostly, "Hi, I am so-and-so, vote for me."

Jen Sharpe
Voter
Phoenix, Arizona

If they talk about their goals and aspirations, it is interesting. If they just say "vote for me," it is annoying.

Jonathan Neal Kassebaum
Voter
San Diego, California

Focus not on what you've been involved in or how popular you are, but on what you intend to do once elected.

Christopher F. Heck
Voter
Fairborn, Ohio

One thing that definitely hurts is not taking real issues seriously.

Regan Gregory
Voter
Chattanooga, Tennessee

Most students will be more impressed by a candidate who intends to do something helpful for them than by one who wants to run a "Saved By The Bell" style election. If you can make your voters actually care about what is going on in their school, you're on your way to winning their votes.

Matthew Ellsworth
Voter
New Haven, Indiana

Talk about what you want to change, but word it as diplomatically as possible. When I ran for Class President in eleventh grade, I went over in my speech what I thought the student administration had done wrong the year before and how I would change it. As it turns out, friends of the previous year's President took my comments as a personal attack on him and it swayed their votes away from me. That doesn't mean you should avoid criticizing previous officers, but that you should speak in terms of what you will do, rather than pointing out what a bad job someone else has done.

> *Kris Long*
> *Class Vice-President*
> *Davie, Florida*

You have to know what the audience is looking for. For example, in high school, all anyone wants to hear is about the cool Senior trips you're going to plan, where the prom is going to be, etc. It's about knowing what your audience is interested in.

> *Sara Herman*
> *Co-Governor of dormitory floor*
> *Bloomington, Indiana*

Keep your platform simple (don't try to solve every problem in a 5-10 minute speech). Concentrate on a few issues and stick to those.

> *Jeff McMahon*
> *Freshmen Executive Committee*
> *Baton Rouge, Louisiana*

The candidates who generally get the most support are the ones who speak to a direct subject, not a broad one, and pose a very possible solution. (It takes eyes to notice a problem, but it takes a brain to fix it!)

> *Jason Johns*
> *Voter*
> *Stockton, California*

Everyone usually always has the same goals: to raise money and promote involvement and unity among students. Be more creative with your goals and make them specific. Have a plan on how to reach the goals.

> Lisa Norlander
> Class Vice President
> Cupertino, California

Bring up examples of things to change that people would be like, "oh yeah, that does kinda piss me off..."

> Brett R. Laurence
> Senior Class Treasurer
> Kennett Square, Pennslyvania

Have some ideas of programs that you might want to do. Not just "I think we should volunteer," but "I talked to the people at... and if I am elected, we can go volunteer there."

> Stephan Fraser
> Voter
> El Paso, Texas

These two people running together made campaign promises that seemed very attractive, but were also POSSIBLE. Others were promising better things, but the student body knew that the headmaster wouldn't approve the things they wanted. Some things the winning team promised included more activities, booking better people to appear at assemblies, and continuing programs that the last class president had already started. Even though some of their ideas weren't entirely original, it was good to know that they recognized and would continue to run some of the good programs that had already gotten started.

> Juan M. Gomez
> Voter
> New York, New York

Concentrate on the issues at hand, never say things simply because you think your audience wants to hear them. This is where one girl who was running for Junior Class President screwed up. Instead of telling the audience what she would try to do as President, she stood up and relied on her cheerleading/ popularity and said, "Most of you know me by now, I'm (name), and I wanna make our Junior year the best EVER! Yeah!" A few moments later, another girl got up and told everyone that she was open to any suggestions that we had to make it a great year, but at the time she was particularly focused on getting the number of absentee days raised (because the teachers had more than the students and everyone was sick from the construction going on in school at the time). She addressed everyone as intelligent human beings and relied purely on their judgment, not outrageous claims or popularity. Needless to say, she became our President.

Michelle Girton
Senior Class Treasurer
Levittown, Pennsylvania

> ## But don't promise something you can't deliver.

Don't put things in your campaign speech about things you want to do to make the school a better place that are IMPOSSIBLE. I hate that. It is so annoying to hear these ideas that everyone knows will never take place.

Martina M. Bills
Voter
Mt. Lebanon, Pennsylvania

NEVER LIE. If you are going to promise something to your fellow classmates, make sure that you have talked to the school board and they agree to let you follow through with your promise... We once had Class Rep's elections, and the student running for President promised in his speech that if he was elected that he would make sure that the entire middle school would receive bigger lockers. Do you think it happened? No. He had not even consulted the board about it.

> Charity Templeton
> Senior Class Secretary
> Cedarville, Arkansas

A candidate digs his/her own grave by making promises to the voters that they possibly cannot fulfill. Example: promising to allow longer lunch periods and candy machines in every hall. Whatever! That's so annoying.

> Amber Dunnam
> Student Council Representative
> Lubbock, Texas

Don't get too wild with the promises that can't be held up, ya know? By the time people are in high school, they can pretty much see through liars and people who exaggerate too much. It's always been a major turn off to me when I'm listening to someone's speech and I can't even begin to believe what they are saying because it's too crazy to happen.

> Sean Falls
> Voter
> Glenview, Ilinois

I like platforms which are believable, not the ones where they say they'll change the school in ways they can't, like making shorter classes and longer lunches and crap like that. (That is what you find the most popular kids saying!)

Michael Price
Voter
Vienna, Virginia

Our current President talked about how her aunt worked in the GAP office and she could get us wholesale clothing to sell as fundraisers. It wasn't true and people were really mad after she got elected and didn't do it.

Lisa Haney
Junior Class Treasurer
Easthampton, Massachusetts

People remember when you have lied to them.

Satyen Saraswat
Mu Alpha Theta State President
Murfreesboro, Tennessee

Don't offer false promises. Those who say that they will cut down on homework before Spring Break, etc. are full of s*** and the students know it.

Angela Lam
Publicity Manager
Toronto, Ontario

Don't make huge promises. I remember two people were running one year, one of whom promised all types of things. The other, who ended up winning, said to us, "I can't promise I will get days shortened or homework lessened. But I can listen to what the students have to say and pass it to the faculty. I will try my best to fulfill any student requests. If that isn't good enough, then I am not the person to elect. But the only promise I can make is I will try my hardest to help you, the students." The other kid couldn't believe he had lost after making all the promises he had.

Jared Della Rocca
Voter
South Huntington, New York

Most campaign speeches are boring. Make yours fun!

Make the speech funny. Nothing works quite like that. If you kind of poke fun at yourself, it's good, if the person who introduces you is hilarious, even better. But it's the funny speeches that are memorable. Those who make them, more often than not, get elected.

Katie McLaughlin
Voter
Royal Oak, Michigan

The more humor you use in speeches, the more people will listen to what you have to say. When campaign speeches are full of facts and figures, students lose interest pretty quickly and don't hear what you need them to. You'll get them to pay attention and remember you if your speech is funny.

Sara Marchant
Voter
Purcellville, Virginia

Humor wins elections. Students will only listen if a speech isn't BORING.

S. Todd Johnson
Voter
Naperville, Ilinois

Most times, people running for office will get up on stage, say their speeches, sit back down, and no one will remember them when voting time rolls around. A candidate must do something to grab the audience's attention so they will remember him/her when it's time to vote.

Jessica Wilson
School Student Council
Clarksburg, West Virginia

Basically, whoever got the audience to laugh during their speeches was the winner.

Lisa Kraft
Student Council Representative
Staten Island, New York

During a campaign speech, my friend Adam commented on the fact that he looked older than everyone else. The speech went something like, "People often look at me and ask, 'you're a Freshman?' I respond, 'yes, I am.' Then they ask, 'you're older than the rest of us, huh?' I respond, 'yes.' Then they just look at me and I respond 'NO'." (As in, people would wonder if he would buy alcohol for them). It was a question which he did often get and the whole audience got a good laugh out of the speech. Overall, he was charismatic, easily heard, and brought the audience into his speech, 3 things which will help any candidate.

Anne Murphy
State House of Reps. Minority Leader
Boston, Massachusetts

During his campaign speech, a student in my class started listing his hobbies. He said, "My hobbies include sports, watching TV, playing Nintendo, and playing with my bird." The entire class began laughing uncontrollably. It was one of the funniest things I've ever heard in an election speech. (The reason it was so funny was because he didn't mean it the way everyone took it. He has a pet bird, but just the way he said it made it hilarious.) Everyone remembered him at voting time and he won.

> *Nick McGuigan*
> *Voter*
> *Plymouth Meeting, Pennsylvania*

If you're willing to embarrass yourself, you're almost sure to win.

> *Michael Bleke*
> *Vice President*
> *Baton Rouge, Louisiana*

It is important to be original so that no one will forget your speech. Even if you make a fool of yourself. You need to leave some impression if you want people to remember you.

> *Shaun Gibson*
> *Voter*
> *Upland, California*

It's all about humor and being very outgoing and outlandish. All that is needed is attention and shock—tasteful shock, of course.

> *Chad Steacy*
> *Junior Class President*
> *Chico, California*

You're a student. Don't be too goody-goody. Don't talk about mundane things like organizing charity bicycle races. You're trying to appeal to one of the most reckless groups in society. Students like to have a laugh. DON'T BE COMPLETELY SERIOUS!!

> *Matt White*
> *Voter*
> *Chartlentree, Britain*

Be creative. Everyone will remember the creativity when they vote, just like a good campaign slogan.

> *Anna Russell*
> *Voter*
> *Fairfax, Virginia*

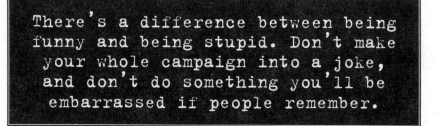

There's a difference between being funny and being stupid. Don't make your whole campaign into a joke, and don't do something you'll be embarrassed if people remember.

It's cool to give a fun speech, but don't make it too ridiculous, cause then it turns people off.

> *Sara Sunflower*
> *Voter*
> *Mesa, Arizona*

People who can never be serious do make the race amusing, but they rarely get elected. I remember a particular line in one speech, taken from JFK's famous speech, "Ask not what your country can do for you..." Only in this speech it became, "Ask not what your school can do for you, but ask what your school can do for me!" I'm sure he was kidding, but still, he didn't win.

> *Emiley L. Erb*
> *Voter*
> *Chesapeake, Virginia*

One guy last year sang a song, but it was incredibly DUMB, so I didn't vote for him. It's fine to do something like that—as long as you do it WELL.

> *Erika A. Bjornson*
> *Voter*
> *Kennewick, Washington*

There was a very popular cheerleader who ran for President and during her speech came out wearing a very respectable outfit, with her hair up and everything. Then, during parts of her speech, she talked about being full of school spirit, and took off her outfit, and under it was her cheerleading uniform. Then she went on to say how she was all for school sports, and took off the cheerleading outfit and had on her track suit. Then she went on to say that if she got elected she would still make time for fun, and stripped down to her bikini. She was NOT looked at very well among students and faculty, and did not even come close to winning.

> *Kristen Koplin*
> *Voter*
> *Vancouver, Washington*

Don't use stupid stunts in your speech. One guy at my school had the last name of Fisher, and he wanted to show everyone that he would do anything for the school, so he swallowed a LIVE goldfish. Not only was this gross, it turned people off majorly. No one wants an idiot for a leader.

David Pearce
Student Body President
Murfreesboro, Tennessee

TALK TO PEOPLE AND ASK THEM TO VOTE

It's the STUDENTS who will be voting. Go meet them!

When people see a ballot, they look for people they know. The more you are known, the better. Be friendly to EVERYONE, even the most unpopular people in school.

Paul Helmbrecht
Voter
Wellington, Montana

The only students who voted were the ones who either knew the candidates or had heard them speak. Candidates should really try to get out and speak about their individual platforms, making themselves known and available.

Emily Wood
Voter
Manasquan, New Jersey

I was running against a very popular girl in my class. I believe that I won because I was more "seen" by more people in general. While she was very popular in my class, I was more visible to the younger grades and I was always nice to them. The girl I was running against was nice to them during her campaign, but she never had been before and I think they were able to see through that. Be aware of the people who are going to be voting.

Emily Stoufer
Student Council President
Nunda, New York

The girl who ran against me was a lot like me, except she wasn't a very friendly person at all, except when it came time for students to vote. I've seen a lot of elections where the best person for the job didn't get elected because they were just shy or something and people never really got to know them. It's hard but you almost have to be a people person so that people won't think that you'll be too shy to push for things.

Megan Statom
Student Council President
Lancaster, Kentucky

Be sure you take every opportunity to meet the people you expect to vote for you!!!! The more people you know the better!!!!!

Lisa Danser
Student Body Secretary
Gastonia, North Carolina

Everybody wants someone they know running the show.

Matt Castleman
Voter
Morgan Hill, California

There is always some popular kid running, but the majority of the student body isn't in the popular crowd, they just happen to know the kids that are and would prefer to vote for someone they've heard of. But if you take your time to meet people and get to know them, you'll find that their votes can be easily altered.

Jennifer Galipault
Student Council Treasurer
Fort Lauderdale, Florida

Talk to everyone. Just say hi to the kids who you don't really know, but know who they are. Say hi to the kids who aren't popular, and you'll gain their respect.

S. Kyle Overstreet
Student Council President
White Oak, Texas

It's time to meet THE OTHER PEOPLE IN THE SCHOOL. It's most likely that you hang around your clique and you are pretty liked so you think that you will definitely win, but actually there are other groups that have their most popular person too. The thing to do is be a good friend to EVERYBODY instead of being best friends with three people. Intermingle and meet people.

Tiffany Noell Gilbreath
Vice President
Birmingham, Alabama

A girl who ran for Senior Class President was very unlikely to win because nobody saw her as popular. She did win, and by a very large margin. What was her secret? She knew everybody and didn't really realize it. She was just friendly and spoke to people. You don't have to have tons of friends to be popular and you don't have to force yourself upon people. Just be friendly and speak to everyone and they will remember you.

Shelby Olson
Voter
Rapid City, South Dakota

Not elaborate propaganda, or witty slashing of your opponent, but relations, it is all about relations.

Drew Foster
Voter
Baldwinsville, New York

Most of the kids would get up to the microphone and make us promises they knew they could never keep. The other ones just acted dumb, hoping their popularity would compensate. I was never convinced, though, and neither were the other kids. The candidates I've always remembered throughout my years in school are the ones who've made themselves known.

Jennifer Kendra Clark
Voter
Tampa Bay, Florida

You don't have to be friends with everyone to be friendly.

Allow yourself to get past old "barriers"—social, personal, whatever—to at least look like you care about people enough to talk to them and acknowledge their presence.

> *Shannon Hinkle*
> *Class President*
> *Clarksville, Indiana*

Don't be a SNOB (so many times people think they are better than others because they are an elected official). REMEMBER: THE ONLY WAY TO BE A LEADER IS TO BE A SERVANT.

> *David Pearce*
> *Student Body President*
> *Murfreesboro, Tennessee*

A girl in my choir class who was running for office came up to me and said, "Oh, you're the girl in choir that sings the solos, right? Vote for me," and handed me a paper and stuff that had her slogan on it. I didn't vote for her. I think that a person should not just thrust their handouts at everyone, but be open enough to learn people's names and be interested in them, and the person will get more votes.

> *Marisa Ruth Werner*
> *Voter*
> *West Valley City, Utah*

It's important to have personal contact with a lot of people, but it's absolutely crucial that you don't have bad breath, because that really turns people off. See a dentist, brush your teeth, brush your tongue, chew gum, eat mints, whatever. Just don't offend people with your halitosis, it's gross.

> *Jamie Allison Torberts*
> *Voter*
> *Gainesville, Florida*

Be aware of what voters want.
Ask them. Listen to them.

Talking to students about their concerns can help you make campaign promises both that you can fulfill and that everyone will like.

Beth Russo
Freshman Senator
Beaumont, Texas

Go out and learn about the people you're trying to reach. Talk with them, find out what "they" want. Someone might give you a great idea.

Michael Crosswhite
Voter
Belleview, Florida

Maybe send out questionnaires or stop students in the hallway to find out what changes they would like in the student council and around the school.

Claire Leone Bissett
Voter
Perthshire, Scotland

Always integrate the ideas of others into your platform. That way you are on everyone's side. Be a people person, not an icon.

John-Paul Wolf
Student Body Historian
Las Vegas, Nevada

Last year a friend of mine running for Junior Class VP set up a podium with speakers in the quad in the middle of the school. He had on a funky "Cat in the Hat" hat and pointed to people with a cane and just started talking to them as they walked by. He asked them what they wanted from the school and fielded questions then and there. He even got some teachers into the questioning. The way he was himself and got his caring/funny personality across to people was great. It was so unique that no one forgot it come election time. Because of his energy, and how he talked to the students, he won.

Charles Lock
Voter
Lexington, Massachusetts

A student at my school announced that he was going to sit at a table in the cafeteria, hall, or other public and easily accessible place so that he could get input, ideas, even criticisms from the students so he knew what needed to be done. I thought this was an excellent idea.

Christina Littlefield
Voter
Hampton, Virginia

One thing that worked in our recent sorority elections, was a girl in our house e-mailed all the other girls, and asked for suggestions, which showed genuine interest.

Christine Yorkshire
Voter
Northbrook, Illinois

Never ignore them or beg them to vote for you, just be nice and really listen to what they are saying, it makes them feel good, and it makes them feel more comfortable around you and sometimes it even causes them to look up to you.

Todd Stewart
Voter
Tampa, Florida

I would have to say that the people who had the most success were the people who actually talked to individuals. If the candidate can get their ideas and beliefs clearly across to even a handful of people, then the snowball effect kicks in. I think that candidates make the assumption that whoever makes the most friends will win, however, this is not always true. I found it an insult to my intelligence when candidates would speak down to me (the audience) and bring in issues that were irrelevant. The most efficient candidate would take informal polls of what issues the voters felt were most important, and then determine what he/she could do about those issues.

Rachael Lennon
Voter
Issaquah, Washington

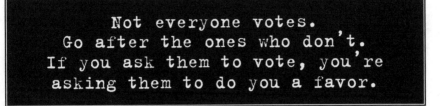

Not everyone votes.
Go after the ones who don't.
If you ask them to vote, you're
asking them to do you a favor.

Talk to everybody you know about voting for you. Even if people are your friends, they may be just too lazy to vote. You have to keep reminding them to vote for you, but in a way that's tactful and not annoying.

Joshua Stern
Senior Class President
Poughkeepsie, New York

Students don't like having to spend part of their lunch period waiting in a line to vote.

Michael Lin
Voter
Millsbrae, California

You will have the best chance by bringing out the people who would normally not vote.

Ben Vandaley
Voter
Rapid City, South Dakota

Get the people who don't care either way to vote for you (the people who just don't care in general).

Sam S. Fleming
Social Chairman of Latin Club
Huntsville, Alabama

I think the biggest thing in getting elected is getting people to know who you are. Stickers and posters and stuff is all good, but I think you need to be in touch with the people. You can win hundreds of votes from people that have no clue what they are doing. It sounds stupid, but go for the kids who don't speak English or the kids who don't give a damn. You'll see that they are more likely to vote for you than the average "popular kid." The main thing is to get people to know you, especially the, shall we say, losers, because their vote counts for a lot.

Maynard James Keenan
Middle School President
Bedford, Massachusetts

On the day of the election, a friend of mine who was helping my campaign went to every table and asked every person if they had voted yet. If they hadn't, he dragged them up to the polls. He didn't ask who they had voted for, just if they had voted at all.

Lauren Stewart
SGA Vice-President of Student Concerns
Kansas City, Missouri

Many schools publish phone books with every student's phone number in them. The night before the election, I called up every single person in the book (even those I thought would not support me) and asked for their support the next day. It took me a very long time (about five hours), and I had a few long distance calls. It was definitely worth it though. Nothing shows your dedication more than this personal touch.

Joshua Karns
Student Council President
Camp Hill, Pennsylvania

The number one reason why I won the election was because my campaign was funny. Everything else was secondary. A large percentage of the class is apathetic to the outcome of the election anyway. By posting funny signs and making the whole campaign something that was fun and amusing to witness, I got the votes of people who usually probably wouldn't even vote.

> *Joshua Stern*
> *Senior Class President*
> *Poughkeepsie, New York*

Get people involved in helping your campaign.

Have a friend or relative in school help with your campaign (the more the merrier) and pass your name around school.

> *Tina M. Yauger*
> *Voter*
> *Fairfield, Ohio*

A thing that helped me to win the election was I made sure I gave my friends jobs to do, so they felt involved and connected to my campaign, and if I was to be elected, then they knew that they put me there, and their support would not be forgotten. Students don't want to elect someone that they think is above them, or better than them. They want someone they know will listen to them, and that they feel comfortable confronting.

> *Jarrett Fisher*
> *Student Body President*
> *Bakersfield, California*

You should try to have friends from all different "groups." If you have intellectual friends, they can help you on speeches and if you have popular friends they can get their friends to vote for you. If you have friends that goof off all the time, they can create humor in your speeches and help give you personality.

> *Derrick Leonard*
> *Secretarial Candidate*
> *Bristol, Tennessee*

Some advice I could give is "treat everyone like somebody." Nobody wants to feel unimportant and not useful. Make a point to get anyone you can involved in your campaign, have them pass out flyers, stickers, candy, etc. Then, whether you win or lose, make sure to thank each of them personally for their help.

> *David Pearce*
> *Student Body President*
> *Murfreesboro, Tennessee*

Use your friends. Ask for their help in making posters, passing out campaign items and spreading the word.

> *Daniel Colton*
> *Student Body President*
> *Scottsdale, Arizona*

GETTING YOUR NAME REMEMBERED

POSTERS

Nobody ever votes for a
name they don't recognize.
Posters should remind everyone
that you're running.

The most important thing is to get your name out there. The truth is, after being bombarded with an hour of campaign speeches littered with empty promises, most students cannot even remember who is running or who said what. When they finally get the ballots, they mark the name they recognize. So you must emphasize your name. They won't vote for you if they can't remember your name.

Jason Miller
Voter
Clovis, California

The biggest thing in an election was the exposure the student received. Normally, I didn't know most of the students on the ballot and I would just pick the ones I remembered or someone said to vote for. Popularity isn't a big deal, it's more like how well the person is known.

Michela Mary Sanders
Voter
Evansville, Indiana

It is not all words and charm, it is the way the people remember you.

Victoria Johnson
Voter
Ft. Walton Beach, Florida

I've never known one person who was influenced by a flashy poster.

Nicholas H. Grainger
Voter
Richmond, Virginia

I only voted for people who put up posters, which meant that some of my best friends, I did not vote for. If someone can't even take the time to make a couple of posters, then they probably aren't going to take much time with normal activities such as homecoming.

Katie Sup
Member of Senior Senate
Omaha, Nebraska

Post interesting things in clever places.

Posters are only as valuable as their location.

Robert O'Brien
Senior Council Senator
Portland, Maine

Do not place the fliers or whatever every five feet, try and get people you know and who are friends to put your fliers up on their lockers. The rest should be in places where people stop walking and do look around. (Often you see the posters in places where you never see them if you walk normally.)

Ben Vandaley
Voter
Rapid City, South Dakota

It gets really boring to drive by all the red, white and blue signs that say, basically, "vote for me." You do not see Nike advertising with boring colors. The reason they are so successful is because of their good marketing. Come on, get creative!

AJ Renchin
Secretary, National Honor Society
Lakeville, Minnesota

Don't post papers everywhere that only say VOTE FOR ME, instead put a quality on it that would suggest why you feel it should be you (and put a different quality on each one).

Jason Johns
Voter
Stockton, California

When you make signs to put up all over the school, put up some reminder of your platform. The group that won had their platform on the walls, while the rest just had little rhyming posters (i.e., "vote so and so, we'll put on a show," things like that).

George Schneider
Voter
New York, New York

Get your poster noticed from among the sea of posters.

The best idea you can have for your poster is: ATTENTION GRABBING! Just make sure you draw them in first...then worry about saying something (if anything other than your name and office you are running for). Don't make it tasteless or REALLY UGLY... but make it jump out at them... sometimes something as simple as using COLORS rather than black and white on the poster can mean getting someone's attention and NOT GETTING IT!

Jon Perillo
Voter
Casey, Ilinois

Chances are, your school will be covered with other people's posters too, so be creative when displaying yours! Try hanging them sideways, upside down, and at imperfect angles. Maybe get some heavy duty duct tape and tape your message to the hallway floor (people will always look down). Hang them above water fountains, in bathroom stalls, and in lunch lines, places where people will look.

Micki Wrangler
Voter
Buffalo, New York

The most effective posters are ones that exhibit some sense of humor. A play on words, especially with the candidate's name, no matter how far stretched or lame, does help a voter remember a name. Also, it is a good idea to omit illustrations which often end up being too cutesy or unrelated and fancy type faces which are hard to read.

Emily Carroll & Alex Ejsmont
School President and Vice President
Toronto, Ontario

Miscellaneous

People will always go for a familiar name rather than an unknown one, even if they have never met the person—so have flyers, buttons, and even pens made with your name streaked across them, to make your name familiar.

Danny Quiroz
Voter
McAllen, Texas

But don't be annoying! This girl in my high school made over 500 posters. They were everywhere. (I went to a small private school, only 250 students, one hallway long). She ran two years in a row and never won.

Kelly A. Adams
Voter
Bucks County, Pennsylvania

Don't spend tons of money for this position. In the eighth grade, a girl wanted to be Class President so her mom gave her three hundred dollars for the campaign. She bought pencils, magnets, buttons, ribbons, and made tons of fliers for this election, and the amount of crap that was then in the halls afterwards... People went out to vote against her so that she wouldn't get elected because they were sick of it all.

Ben Vandaley
Voter
Rapid City, South Dakota

One of the guys who was running for President made tons of buttons that said "Vote for Hunter." He had scanned famous scenes from movies into his computer, like where Forrest Gump meets the President, or a scene from the Wizard of Oz, and superimposed his picture into the scene. He made hundreds of these buttons, and distributed them to the entire student body. As it grew nearer to election day, he would show up in the outfits he was wearing in the button pictures, like a flag print top hat, a blazer, and flag print boxer shorts. Everyone in the school was talking about what he was wearing, and it was great publicity for him. I think he was able to show the student body that he was dedicated to being their President by his willingness to make a complete fool of himself. It worked, though, because he won the election.

Lindsey Wortham
Club Vice President
Austin, Texas

Don't use paint to make your posters if there is a chance of rain. Big mistake.

Daniel Colton
Student Body President
Scottsdale, Arizona

HANDOUTS

What can you hand out?

Make up a survey and put in the teachers' boxes and ask the teachers to pass them out and collect them. Then announce the results and do what the students want.

Robert Craft
Voter
Jacksonville, Florida

The cutest speech was all designed around candy that would be tossed into the crowd by two very cute guys. She told of how she wouldn't get BUTTERFINGERS in office or wouldn't SNICKER at anyone's ideas, she had WHOPPERS of ideas, and things along those lines.

Jaclyn Houghton
Executive Board Treasurer
Urbandale, Iowa

A kid gave his speech and said "and anyone who doesn't want to vote for me or isn't convinced they should... Suck on this..." and he tossed out suckers to the crowd...

Teresa M. Robinson
Student Council Vice-President
Bethany, West Virginia

Write "Stick with (name)" on little slips and tape them on Pixie Sticks to pass out.

Rachel Spear
French Club President
Bay St. Louis, Missouri

One of my best friends ran for Class President every year. Last year, she passed out "Vote for Kasee" gum! It was really creative and cute! She made her own labels and basically just taped them on. It wasn't anything fancy, but the student body liked it!

Emily Bildstein
Student Representative
Marion, Iowa

Some "bribes" I have seen are personalized pencils that say "Sally Field for Vice-President." They are very eye-catching. I also have found that stickers and buttons work well too, because it shows that the person is advertising him/herself aggressively and really wants to win.

Navneet Sandhu
Voter
Clifton, Virginia

It seemed the people who handed out things such as pencils, notepads, etc. would have an edge because you look at that stuff time and time again, whereas stuff like candy, you just eat.

Alecia Frisby
Class President
Ellicott City, Maryland

What worked for campaigns in elementary was giving out stuff. I passed out pencils with a piece of paper that had my name on it attached. I didn't pass out candy because the teachers didn't like it, and if the kids got candy from one of the candidates, they thought they were really cool but changed their minds after the teacher took the candy away or the kid got in trouble. Another good thing about the pencils is that if they use them, not only do they see your name all day long, but so do the people around them.

Alison Comstock
Voter
Houston, Texas

Bribery

I have one word for you: CANDY! Candy was always the thing that swayed my vote. If the dork gives me the candy and the cool kid gives me some lame slogan, I would vote for that dork in a heartbeat. I do know a girl who had many friends and she was up against a nobody and she lost because he gave out the candy. The candy that wins the most votes is the Charms blow pop, pass a few of those bad boys around with a sticker that has your name on it and you are a shoo-in!

Elizabeth Hayward Wagner
Voter
Grosse Pointe South, Michigan

Bribery—unfortunately, it works. A Jolly Rancher will go farther than a button in most high schools. People want something for nothing—they see elections as another opportunity to get something. But be smart—if most people resort to bribery, candy is the easiest medium. Since most people will be using candy—what is going to make you stand out? What I have found effective was wrapping the Jolly Rancher with a piece of paper taped around it. To get to the bribe (the candy), they have to get though the paper. Man by nature is curious. It is safe to say that most people will open it up and find out what the piece of paper says. On the Jolly Ranchers I have used, my paper has had some cartoons on them—cartoons using slogans to help me. Sure, this will take some time—but so will the office which you want to occupy. It's a good project to ask your friends to help you with.

Satyen Saraswat
Mu Alpha Theta State President
Murfreesboro, Tennessee

My Senior year, I ran for Vice-President of my choir class, and to get people's votes, my friend Philip (who was running for President) and I passed out suckers!!!!! Well we WON!!!!!!! People will vote for anyone who is giving them something!! It makes you kind of sad...

Heather Vorhoff
Vice-President of Concert Choir
Garden City, Michigan

I passed out pencils (#2 of course) and put labels on them that said "Mark your ballot for Mary Beth." Unfortunately, the student body found Andes Mints more appealing than pencils...

Mary Beth Harrison
President, National Honor Society
Hull, Georgia

Giving stuff away doesn't guarantee votes.

Don't waste your time with candy or any bribing tools, because it doesn't work. I ran against a girl who bribed everyone, and they ate her candy and voted me in.

Christopher J. Collins
Student Council President
Corpus Christi, Texas

Trying to bribe people for votes doesn't work. Like bringing the whole school chocolate chip cookies—people will only use you for a short while then pretend they don't know you come election time.

Tina M. Yauger
Voter
Fairfield, Ohio

My slogan for the regular election was "Don't Be a Dum-Dum, Vote Jennifer for Student Council President" and I put Dum-Dum lollipops on all of the tables in the lunch room with a little tag attached with the slogan, reminding them to go down and vote. I also stood right outside the voting poll and handed out my Dum-Dums and reminded them to vote for the best candidate, me!... For the run-off election, my slogan was "Jennifer Always Keeps her Promises..." and I handed out Dove's Promises candies at lunch again and put some at each lunchroom table. Although I did not win the election...

Jennifer Bailey
Vice President of Florida Association of
Student Councils
Fort Meade, Florida

> ```
> Beware: attempting to
> bribe voters can backfire.
> ```

Something that a girl did in her A.S.B. campaign that I thought caused her to lose the election was pass out suckers at lunchtime. I thought it was terrible campaigning. Before she did that, I was planning to vote for her, but after she did it, I changed my mind and a lot of people I know did too.

Jennifer L. Stair
Voter
Kennewick, Washington

A girl who was running for Class President gave away Smarties. All of the people she gave them to ended up dropping them on the floor and grinding them into the carpet. She didn't win, and she had to clean up the mess. It's actually sort of a sad story...

Kristina Moran
Voter
Kilgore, Texas

Make sure to find out your school's rules on giving out candy and such before you necessarily do it, because you might get yourself disqualified.

Jeremy Gorelick
Club President
Greenlawn, New York

Dropping a little money never hurt, but it can work two ways. When I ran for Student Body President last year, I went all out. I'm talking pens, bumper stickers, banners, the works. Getting my name around worked pretty well, and I came within 25 votes of upsetting a rather popular incumbent. As the campaign wore on, though, I became aware of a "money backlash." This is a situation unique to the high school election where people get sick of seeing your name all over the place and vote for the other guy just because he is less exposed.

Kyle Rossi
Class Treasurer
Solon, Ohio

PART 4

FINAL NOTE

FINAL NOTE

THE TOP TEN WAYS TO WIN A HIGH SCHOOL ELECTION:

10. Don't give up by not trying. PUSH YOURSELF to *go for it!*

9. Don't overdo it with the posters, they're not what people base their votes on. KEEP THE PUBLICITY CUTE AND SIMPLE, and *focus instead on being the most genuine, approachable, easy-going candidate running—be a "people person."*

8. Keep the ATTITUDE that *you're just a typical, normal student, a peer* who wants to work hard for the class and who has concrete ideas and real enthusiasm for the job. Do not get self-important or act political. Do *not* plastic-smile and kiss babies.

7. Be friendly and TALK TO EVERYONE, not just the popular people. Hang around in the hallways and meet the students, don't turn your back on them to hang more posters.

6. ASK PEOPLE TO VOTE. Especially the people who normally wouldn't vote at all. The person with the most support doesn't win, *the person with the most votes* does. Get them to the polls!

5. Keep your campaign speech SHORT. All the candidates are qualified, so don't list all your credentials. *Quickly* show that you're fun, that you have ideas, that you're sincere, and that you want the job, and then *shut up and sit the heck down.*

4. Have a FUNNY campaign speech. Nothing wins the attention of high school students like humor. Don't be too silly, but don't be too serious. Ask your friends to help you write your speech, and PRACTICE beforehand, because preparation is the key to conquering nerves. *Funny speeches usually win school elections.*

3. Don't be fake, JUST BE YOURSELF.

2. Don't be fake, JUST BE YOURSELF.

1. Don't be fake, JUST BE YOURSELF.

IF YOU REMEMBER ONLY ONE THING FROM THIS BOOK, I HOPE IT IS THIS:

High school elections—as with most things in life—are *not necessarily fair.* They're not necessarily objective. The best person doesn't always win. Striving to be a nice, friendly, genuine person who others *like* and *want to support* will get you further than almost anything else.

The author loves getting any kind of feedback.

Do you have advice or an idea which should be included here?

Please email JeffMarx@schoolelection.com

This book is independently published, which means

it's not extensively (expensively) advertised.

If you have friends who you think could benefit from

this book, please direct them to www.schoolelection.com.

If you have a website, PLEASE link to mine.

Banners and commissions are available.

See www.schoolelection.com/link2us.html

You don't need to be helped any longer.

Glinda, the Good Witch of the North

RAP

5-15-00

GAYLORD FG